Y0-AIY-029

Strindberg

Three Experimental Plays

STRINDBERG

THREE EXPERIMENTAL PLAYS

Translated with an Introduction

by

F. R. Southerington

University Press of Virginia

Charlottesville

The University Press of Virginia

Copyright © 1975 by the Rector and Visitors
of the University of Virginia

First published 1975

All rights reserved. Except for brief
passages quoted in a newspaper, magazine,
radio, or television review, no part of
this book may be reproduced in any form
or by any means, including photocopying
and taping, without permission of the
translator.

All inquiries concerning rights, pro-
fessional and amateur, should be
addressed to F. R. Southerington, Mary
Baldwin College, Staunton, Virginia
24401.

The publication of Strindberg: Three
Experimental Plays was sponsored by
Mary Baldwin College.

Library of Congress Cataloging in Publication Data

Strindberg, August, 1849-1912
   Three experimental plays.

   CONTENTS: Miss Julie.--The stronger.--A dream
play.
   1. Title.
PT9811.A3S56   1975   838.7'2'6   74-19142
ISBN 0-8139-0605-9

Printed in the United States of America

FOREWORD

An agreeable translation for actors is an essential prerequisite for the satisfactory expression of a foreign play and of its author's intention. The historical fact is that often, notably in the cases of Ibsen and Strindberg, the first translations of foreign plays into English have been either literal or literary rather than theatrical. Although the plays in spite of this basic handicap attracted audiences because of the trenchant posture of the playwrights, that posture was wildly misinterpreted, as with Ibsen's <u>A Doll's House</u> and nearly every play of Strindberg's.

Such misinterpretations can usually be traced to arthritic translations that could be used in the theater only by overcompensating in subsidiary aspects of the production. This unhappy state of affairs may indeed have been what brought Ibsen to his humiliating compromise of a happy ending to the first German production of <u>A Doll's House</u>. Dr. Southerington's brilliant exegesis of the Strindberg plays in this volume has its premise in translating for actors and in revising during his production experience of these three plays. Without this orientation neither his explications nor his translations would have so clearly surpassed those of his predecessors.

Every verbal composition loses something in translation. By striving for what "lies right" for actors, for what "works," for what plays well, Dr. Southerington has reduced to a minimum the amount of loss in transmission of Strindberg's plays into English. He avoids such temptations to modernize or anglicize as converting Swedish

Jean or Kristin to John or Christine. The Swedish flavor is retained, but the rhythms of the dialogue are genuinely English.

Another source of Dr. Southerington's superior translations and explications of Strindberg is his familiarity with the playwright's life. As a forthcoming biographer of Strindberg, with access to much hitherto unavailable material, he is able to judge more astutely Strindberg's intentions and therefore to represent his subject's dialogue and characterizations more accurately. Until now Strindberg's English readers and audiences have hardly suspected the considerable comic intent of such a grandly philosophical drama as A Dream Play.

Fletcher Collins, Jr.

ACKNOWLEDGMENTS

I have received much practical help from Mary Baldwin College, particularly from the Mary Baldwin College Drama Department; from the Oak Grove Theater and Theater Wagon, Staunton, Virginia, and especially from their founders and inspirers, Fletcher and Margaret Collins; from friends in Sweden who have kindled my enthusiasm for Strindberg and discussed the texts, particularly Kerstin and Lennart Lindström; from successive students of Ibsen and Strindberg at Mary Baldwin College, most notably Mary Warren Montague, whose own views of Strindberg will, I hope, reach the published page; and from the large company of friends and actors who have helped me put these plays on stage and let me hear these lines spoken in their proper context.

Most of all, I have been helped by the support of my wife Terry, who has borne with me as these plays were translated, has been an admirable producer time and time again, and has typed this manuscript with dedication and without complaint.

The passage from Schopenhauer quoted in the Introduction is from *The World as Will and Idea*, translated by R. B. Haldane and J. Kemp, London, 1883, Vol. III, p. 382.

CONTENTS

Foreword by Fletcher Collins, Jr.   v

Acknowledgments   vii

Introduction   xi

Miss Julie   1

The Stronger   47

A Dream Play   53

INTRODUCTION

AUGUST STRINDBERG

Johan August Strindberg was born in Stockholm on January 22, 1849. Sensitive and precocious, he had a difficult childhood whose most crucial event was probably the death of his mother in 1862. From her he had derived tenderness and protection against an authoritarian father, and under the influence of her memory his attitudes to women ranged from reverence for the madonna to contempt for the whore. Rarely, if ever, did he see women simply as women, and never did he see them as companions. He kept few friends, male or female, yet those who did come close to him recalled generosity and humor. He was his own best analyst, however, and no subsequent attempts to understand him have improved upon his own self-searching. Explicitly, in a series of autobiographical novels, and implicitly, in almost everything he wrote, Strindberg offers us the self-portrait of tortured and unstable genius, whose fluctuating experiments in belief are in themselves a composite history of nineteenth-century opinion. Buckle, Spencer, Darwin, Kierkegaard, Nietzsche, Ibsen, Zola, Swedenborg, with others, all at one time earned his respect and at others his contempt. He rarely adopted any belief or lifestyle for long, and he saw each phase of his career only as an experiment to discover meaning and satisfaction in human life. It is doubtful whether he found either.

Strindberg was relieved to find escape from his childhood home into the freedom of university life. But as a student at Uppsala in 1867 he found only the freedom to starve. For the next few years he led a precarious existence, part student, part teacher, part medical apprentice. He made his first attempts as a dramatist, and one play, The Outlaw, was performed and even earned him a short-lived royal stipend. His debut as an actor was a fiasco. For a while he edited an insurance journal which dissolved into bankruptcy. Not until 1874, when he was appointed secretary at the Royal Library in Stockholm, did he find any measure of financial or emotional security.

It did not last long. In 1875 he first met Baroness Siri von Essen Wrangel. After a tumultuous courtship, culminating in her divorce and her pregnancy, he married her in 1877. Siri had ambitions, and some talent, as an actress, but in the years that followed she was given only a little opportunity to develop her talent. The birth of three children, and a continuous pilgrimage through Europe, with periods of residence in France and Switzerland, meant that Strindberg quickly forgot his earlier promises. Strindberg's self-centeredness, and his growing suspicions of Siri, brought friction into their marriage and, to Strindberg, an increasing sense of guilt. Matters grew worse when in 1884 he was summoned to appear in Stockholm on a charge of blasphemy growing out of his collection of short stories, Married. After some hesitation he appeared for the trial and was triumphantly acquitted; but the nervous strain had been acute and was reflected in even greater instability than before. After living in Switzerland, France, Bavaria, and Denmark, the Strindbergs returned to Sweden and a racking divorce in 1891.

Within two years Strindberg was married again, this time to Austrian-born Frida Uhl; within another three years he was again divorced. His own account of the years that followed, Inferno, begins with his separation from his second wife, and documents meticulously the pattern of delusions, hallucinations, and persecution-complex from which he sought continuously and unsuccessfully to escape. Whatever the clinical diagnosis--and I have seen no wholly convincing clinical analysis--Strindberg was, by ordinary standards, mad. This was the most agonized period of his life, but it proved to be the richest source of his creativity. More than half of his life's work was written after the Inferno period. All of it, most particularly the To Damascus trilogy, dramatizes the suffering and self-questioning of a self-tormented spirit, and records the religious conversion which emerged. Like everything else about Strindberg, the religious beliefs he adopted were highly individual; but the conversion was genuine, and the mixture of resignation and compassion which it embodies informs and ennobles the greatest works of his later years. In A Dream Play most of all, Strindberg offers a fatalistic understanding of man's suffering, softened by humor and a gentle and melancholy tenderness. His attempts to impose form upon the world of dream and the irrational which he had come to know so well were to place him at the forefront of the European theater.

A third marriage, to the young Danish actress Harriet Bosse in 1901, was followed by a third divorce in 1904. This time, though the experience was no less painful, Strindberg was coming to terms with his own self-contradictions, and there was no final breach with Harriet until her remarriage to a young actor in 1907. But if the private Strindberg had mellowed a little, the public man had not. In The Red Room of 1879 Strindberg had confronted Sweden with a biting social criticism which had alarmed some and delighted others; now they were again lashed by his ferocious contempt, and the last few years were surrounded by the controversy of the "Strindberg feud." For years Sweden had ignored him; now his European reputation made him impossible to ignore. After his death from cancer of the stomach in 1912, his funeral procession was followed by thousands of workers and students who saw him, not entirely accurately, as their champion. Nonetheless, Strindberg never became a member of the Swedish Academy, and he was not awarded the Nobel Prize. Given his contempt for normality and the "status quo," neither distinction would have been much to his taste.

In his art, as in his life, Strindberg could not stand still. He was novelist, poet, and playwright; he was also a painter of considerable distinction, a pioneer of photography, the holder of an Imperial Russian Order for his Sino-Russian studies, and an amateur linguist, chemist, and alchemist. It is our loss that the English-speaking world knows him almost exclusively as a dramatist.

INTRODUCTION   xiii

The three plays offered in translation in this volume were in
their time experimental works. Two of them, Miss Julie and A Dream
Play, have become classics, while The Stronger survives as a tour de
force which retains its challenge even for the most experienced actress.
The translations are not intended to be "literary": that is, they
are translations, not transliterations. They are intended to be
spoken in performance, rather than read in the classroom. Each of
them has been tested in production and subsequently amended where
necessary. This does not mean that accuracy has been knowingly sacri-
ficed; it does mean that the plays have been approached as plays,
and not as volumes from the library shelf. I have tried to capture
some of Strindberg's stylistic range, but in doing so I have also
tried to remember that our players need to speak the English language
in a convincing form.

MISS JULIE, THE STRONGER, AND A DREAM PLAY

Miss Julie was written in the early summer of 1888, one of the
more tumultuous years of Strindberg's tumultuous life. His marriage
to Siri von Essen was in ruins, though this did not prevent him from
casting her as Julie in the first private performance of the play
in 1889, nor from becoming fiercely jealous of the young actor who
played opposite her. He had also become scandalously involved with
a seventeen-year-old servant girl whose elder brother was threatening
to make trouble. His financial difficulties were acute. And he was
racked by a sense of sexual inferiority. Nor was he content with
his creative work. He felt himself obliged to write tales of life
in the Stockholm archipelago which, although he affected to despise
them, were to the public taste, instead of reaping the artistic and
financial benefit from The Father, for which the public had no taste
at all. However, his own passing opinion that his mind was merely
lying fallow after the exertions of The Father may have been nearer
the truth; nor did it lie fallow for very long. The Father was written
in 1887. In August, 1888, Strindberg was able to write to publisher
Karl Otto Bonnier:

> I take the liberty of sending herewith the first
> naturalistic tragedy in Swedish drama, and beg you
> not to reject it thoughtlessly, for you would come
> to regret that...this play will live in the annals...

Strindberg was right, but Bonnier rejected the play nonetheless, warning
its author that he would be fortunate if he could find anyone to
perform it. It was, in fact, another eighteen years before Miss
Julie was publicly performed in Sweden, even though its success at
the Freie Bühne in Berlin in 1892, and at the Theatre Libre in Paris
in 1893, had seen Strindberg acknowledged as one of the greatest
playwrights of his day.

The "difficulties" which confronted audiences in the 1890's are
not entirely unfamiliar even now. The brutality and cynicism of Jean's
treatment of Julie are no longer so shocking, but Strindberg's

"naturalism" can still be puzzling to the more literal-minded. In following Zola's appeal for simplicity and truth to reality, Strindberg applied his own concepts of character and motivation. What motivates Julie is not some specific, fixed trait of personality, but a complex of traits aggravated by a specific time and situation. Strindberg was at pains to explain himself in the remarkable preface to the play, and he repeated his explanation elsewhere:

> ...the unconscious reluctance to propagate caused by an impoverished hereditary strain...a weakness in the will to live, the dream of falling from the pillar, the mother's reluctance to have intercourse, the masculine upbringing, and so on. The suicide is properly motivated: lack of will to live, a longing for the end of the race in this last poor individual, the noblewoman's shame at her bestiality with a lower species, and further: the suggestive power of the bird's blood, the proximity of the razor, fear of discovery of the theft, and the orders of a stronger will (first the valet's, and, further off, the Count's). Notice that, left to herself, Julie would have lacked the strength, but now she is driven or led by innumerable motives.
> (Strindberg to Georg Brandes, December 4, 1888)

Obviously not all these motives are actually apparent in the action ("the mother's reluctance to have intercourse," etc.), but in outline Strindberg's analysis is fair. The credibility of the action is established with remarkable economy. Jean's first line, "Miss Julie is crazy tonight, just crazy!," places us at the heart of things, particularly if the sexual connotations of the Swedish _galen_ (crazy, wild, "in heat") are sufficiently suggested by Jean's delivery and directly related to Kristin's observations on the pregnant bitch Diana. Moreover, the use of the peasant interlude, not simply to allow time for the seduction itself, but also to suggest the gaiety and abandon of Midsummer Eve, can of itself create an atmosphere in which Julie's fall is not simply explicable but almost inevitable. The play naturally falls into two parts, before and after the seduction, and to play the first without attention to its gaiety and pace is to lose the mainstream of the action.

It is sometimes observed that the clash of social ranks and the sexual conquest of Jean are now themes too outdated and trivial to offer us a truly tragic sense. It is difficult to answer such criticism, since it mistakes the machinery for the plot. It could also be objected that kings do not divide their realms among their daughters, and our father's ghosts do not return from the dead to exhort us to revenge. Strindberg himself met the criticism with a clear-sighted understanding of his purpose:

> In this play I have not tried to do anything new--that is impossible--but I have tried to modernize the form to meet the demands of modern men.

> To that end I have chosen--or been chosen by--a theme which can be said to lie outside the clash of contemporary opinion. The distinctions between rising and falling social classes, higher or lower, better or worse, men or women, are, have always been, and always will be of abiding interest... I believed the action suitable for tragedy because the extinction of a favored individual, and still more of a favored race, still appeals to the tragic sense...there can be no cheap sneers over a situation which lowers the lid on the coffin of a race.

Strindberg's appeal to form is an attempt to lay bare the "psychological process"--"we want to know how it works." In *Miss Julie* we see two major characters who "work" by their association with one another and with an environment whose normality is represented on the one hand by Kristin and on the other by the absent Count. But their association here is not normal, and the rapidly shifting dialogue in which Jean, for example, can be seen groping for the thread with which he will weave his tissue of lies is an expression of that mental struggle which Strindberg called "the battle of minds." Jean, ultimately, is the stronger not because he represents the future race or the Nietzschean overman--though there are obvious traces of Nietzsche in the characterization of both Jean and Julie--but because he has the stronger and more ruthless will. Strindberg sees Julie's refinement, it is true, as the result of a decayed ancestry; the modern audience, however, while it is prepared to believe for the moment the account of Julie's ancestry, is more convinced by the prospect of a sensitive mind at first fascinated, and finally repelled, by a coarseness whose attraction lies in its unfamiliarity to her nature.

As in *The Father, Creditors,* and *The Stronger,* Strindberg's principal concern is with the role of will in a human existence marked by the struggle for survival. In his essay *Psychic Murder* Strindberg explained his theme:

> ... The struggle for power is no longer purely physical (prison, torture, death), but has developed to become psychic, though no less cruel. Despots once ruled with physical force and armed men; now majorities (or minorities) govern with the help of newspaper articles and the ballot box... In other, more intimate, areas of social life the struggle between minds is just as fierce. We see daily examples of parents who wish to curb certain talents in their children or encourage others which are only rudimentary; children who torment the lives out of their parents by compromising the family name simply to extort money; husbands and wives who struggle for power over money, servants, or children...

Aware, too, that tradition was on his side, he cited several examples, including the most obvious one:

> Iago murders Othello without using rapier or dagger, only by waking his suspicions, which are increased by Desdemona's coquettish conduct, so that she too has a share in the murder, even though she is not a criminal.

He had explored the theme ruthlessly in The Father, where his own description of Othello's death may literally be applied: Laura provokes the Captain's madness and death in exactly the same way as Iago provokes Othello. In Miss Julie Strindberg sought to refine his medium, reducing The Father's three acts to one, preserving the unities of place and time for the sake of verisimilitude, and supplying a sufficiently feverish pace and atmosphere at the opening of the play to render credible the hypnotic state into which Julie eventually falls at the play's end.

That final scene of Miss Julie is already suggestive of the fantasy world of Strindberg's post-Inferno plays. There had been a hint of this already at the beginning of the Father's mental collapse:

> We, everyone, have been living our lives like children, unconscious, and full of fantasies, ideals, and illusions. Until we woke! But we woke with our feet on the headrail in a topsy-turvy world, and the one who woke us was himself a sleepwalker. When women grow old and cease to be women they get beards on their chins. What does a man get when he grows old and ceases to be a man? The cock crowed, but it was no longer a cock but a capon, answered by a flock of sexless hens. And instead of sunrise we found ourselves sitting among ruins in the broad moonlight, just as in the good old days. What we thought was a casual nap was tormented with wild dreams, and there was no awakening!

This is already a voice new to the drama, but motivated in part by the Captain's madness. In Miss Julie we find the heroine possessed of similar fantasies, but with no trace of madness as an explanation:

> I am asleep! The whole room is in smoke. You look like an iron stove--like a dark-clad man in a top hat--and your eyes shine like coals after the flames have gone out--and your face a white blur like fallen ashes--so warm--so cosy--so light--so peaceful.

But by the time Julie has reached this point of departure from the real world we have already seen her brought close to a hypnotic state as Jean describes the fictional experiences of his boyhood. She drops her lilac as he speaks, and has to reassert her sense of reality with the condescending but nervous, "You tell a beautiful story. Did you ever go to school?" In the same defensive manner she follows her own rapt account of her dream and Jean's account of his with

"Here I stand talking about dreams." We have seen Jean provoke her to violence when she slaps his face, and we have seen her own passionate response to the sight of violence as Jean kills the greenfinch: "I'd give anything to see your brains smashed on a wooden block. I'd like to see your whole sex swimming like that in its blood. By God, I'd like to wade knee-deep through your guts..."

What makes this flexibility possible and convincing is Strindberg's extraordinary boldness of dialogue, a range which allows him to show Julie passionately angry, girlishly coquettish, sunk in reverie or reminiscence, or wandering with Kristin in the unreal world of the Swiss hotel. The Julie who virtually sleepwalks to her suicide is compatible with all the Julies we have seen before, chiefly because Strindberg does not allow us simply to see one.

The Stronger is an attempt to take further the simplification of form and the exploration of psychic control. By reducing the number of characters to two, only one of whom is allowed to speak, Strindberg has stretched his form to its final extreme before it disintegrates into monologue. Indeed, with a weak Miss Y the play can become a monologue. But here, as elsewhere, a modern player is well-advised to listen to Strindberg himself, whose understanding of the needs and problems of the actor has rarely been surpassed by a playwright. He writes in his Memorandum to the members of the Intimate Theater:

> The actor who has no lines but is supposed to listen to someone else, must really listen. He cannot look bored, even if he has heard the other's lines a hundred times... I have seen masterpieces of the art of listening and dumb show. In Miss Julie I have seen Jean listen to Miss Julie's long biography as if he were hearing it for the first time, even though he had heard it 150 times before; and in the same play I have seen the cook listen to Julie's deathly fantasies of an imagined happy future in such a way that I had to applaud the cook.

Certainly Miss Y hears enough variation of tone and pace to justify her listening intently, and The Stronger should be a virtuoso piece for both actresses. It is an obvious tour de force for one of them. From her first "Amelia, darling!" Mrs. X is firmly established. But, again, she is not established as a single type. It is rewarding simply to set some of her lines beside one another to gain a sense of her variety:

> Oh, last Christmas, do you remember how happy you were, out there in the country with his parents?

> I would have scratched her eyes out if she'd come near the place while I was home.

> I made you my friend because I was afraid to have you
> as my enemy. I was uneasy when you came to see us, be-
> cause I could see my husband couldn't stand you. I felt
> awkward, as if I were wearing an ill-fitting dress.
>
> Your very soul crept into mine, like a maggot into an
> apple, eating and eating, digging, digging, until all
> you left was a husk and a little mold.
>
> You sit here like some crazy pilot counting shipwrecks,
> receiving every personal disaster as an offering to you.
>
> Thank you, Amelia, for everything you've taught me; and
> thank you for teaching my husband how to love.

Indeed, we watch her learn, and her language changes as the lesson is driven home.

In these plays, and primarily in the two great tragedies, The Father and Miss Julie, Strindberg broke away from the fetters of orthodox characterization, and in The Stronger he took his pursuit of simplified form to its ultimate conclusion. It is tempting to believe that, even without the experiences of the Inferno crisis, his next step would have been to break the bounds of conventional form and the restrictions of plot. It is almost true to say that A Dream Play has no plot. Indra's Daughter visits the earth to see if men's complaints are justified; she discovers that indeed they are, and returns to report to her father. That is all. Yet of all Strindberg's plays, A Dream Play is the most varied.

A Dream Play was written in 1901, with the exception of the prologue for Indra's Daughter, which Strindberg added in 1906. Its first performance took place in Stockholm in 1907. The play contains a rich fantasy based upon Strindberg's personal experiences, especially those from childhood and his three marriages, and its generally pessimistic tone reflects the collapse of his marriage with Harriet Bosse, which took place even as the play was being shaped. Yet the autobiographical features, though interesting, are largely irrelevant. The moods and ideas reflected had long been habitual with Strindberg. What is more important is the control he managed to exercise over such a diversity of material.

Strindberg was proud of the play, but he did not find it easy to write, calling it "the child of my greatest pains." In part this was because he found himself reliving experiences which were distressing; but he had also to endure the artistic pains of discovering a form which would properly convey the dreamlike world in which time and space were as much illusions as everything else.

At first sight, the result is baffling, most of all to a technical director, and productions of A Dream Play have often been badly hampered by stage machinery and elaborate scenery. Strindberg has sometimes been blamed for this. But he had in mind the rapid transitions

INTRODUCTION   xix

of the Shakespearean stage, and he has asked for nothing that cannot be reproduced in the theater with only a little ingenuity and an appeal to the audience's imagination. The play was produced at the Oak Grove Theater, Staunton, Virginia, in the summer of 1973 with only one intermission, and that was a concession to the comfort of the audience, not a response to the demands of the play. The experience of this production was that a combination of set pieces and lighting changes was enough to achieve most of the effects required. We were doing little more, however, than following Strindberg's own instructions to the Intimate Theater, in which he discusses the hazards of too mechanized a production:

> A certain unjustified fear of employing lighting effects, "straight out of the music halls," kept the director from using the very resources we needed. I wanted to watch the prologue, but I could not distinguish the action in the prevailing darkness: when I asked for an overhead light, to see to understand, I was told, "That's for the music hall." Since I had not been to a music hall for thirty-five years I failed to see the danger. I told him, "Never mind the music hall; I can learn anywhere. It was in a circus that I first discovered what surprising effects could be achieved by painting on a transparent backcloth." But the effect of my prologue was ruined. The sets destroyed the actors' reverence for the play, and demanded innumerable breaks in the action; besides which the entire production became a 'material phenomenon,' instead of its intended opposite (Dematerialization). Now, at the Intimate Theater, we are making an entirely new attempt at the Dream Play. But instead of painted sets, which in this instance cannot provide the fleeting and unfixed mirages, we intend to use only the effects of color. We have discovered, for example, that velvet is receptive to every nuance, from sky blue through metallic hues to purple, simply under the influence of different lighting. And instead of today's nondescript dress we have decided to use brightly colored costumes from every period, demanding only that they be beautiful; for in the dream-life realism is not an important question...we intend to use symbolic pieces, merely suggestive of the locale. For example, two large shells suggest the proximity of the sea; two cypresses transport us to Italy; two signal flags in red and blue indicate Foulstrand; a pair of statuettes are Fairhaven...

In fact, the less scenery the better. Color, lighting, and pace are all that are needed to bring A Dream Play to vibrant life, and a stress on the humor of the play will go a long way to make the pace inevitable. One further aid to the impression of "unfixed and fleeting mirages" has become traditional: the doubling of parts among the actors wherever possible, so that the same faces appear in different roles. The Daughter herself is called upon to change character as soon as she sets foot upon the earth, and, even though she is the most stable figure in the play, neither we nor the other characters are ever sure for long whether to see her as the daughter of the gods or as Agnes, daughter of men.

Strindberg's search for the "dream" form had been greatly advanced in the First Part of To Damascus. There the symmetry of plot, in which the entire action leads to and away from a central scene in the Asylum, had offered him a tight framework within which to present the shifting fantasies of a single mind, that of the Stranger. To some extent A Dream Play follows this same method. The play opens and closes outside the castle and, through two scenes at Fingal's Cave, it leads up to and away from the scenes at Foulstrand and Fairhaven. But exact symmetry of pattern is abandoned. We can discern a line down to Foulstrand and up again after Fairhaven, as if the Daughter is sinking deeper and deeper into mortality during the first half of the play, but there is no such clear pattern as we find in To Damascus. This is appropriate, since it is through the Daughter's eyes that we experience this dream-world, and she, like everyone else in the action, is neither the victim nor the agent of any controlled pattern. She is given a coherent purpose, unlike all the other characters except, perhaps, the Poet; but she too can act without motivation, and in her desire to see the opening of the cloverleaf door she follows an illusion as devotedly as the Officer in his yearning for Victoria. Like the others, she is under the illusion that life has meaning. Only with the discovery that the meaning of life is nothing is she free to return to her father.

Instead of a symmetry of form, Strindberg gives us thematic symmetry. The twin themes of Justice and Hope echo endlessly throughout the play, with variation on variation, couched often in richly comic terms. The discovery that Justice and Hope are in themselves illusory would be easily made, were it not that men find illusion easier to bear than reality. As the play reaches its close the major characters abandon some of their false hopes as they cast their illusions to the flames; but the Billsticker may fairly claim to express the reservations of all of them. "These notices may go, but my fishnet--never!" Only for the Daughter and the Poet is there a complete understanding:

> Look at everything the sea has robbed and crushed.
> So many ships sunk, and only the figureheads remain!
> And the names...Justice, Friendship, Golden Peace,
> Hope--this is all that remains of Hope, treacherous Hope!

The Daughter's life on earth is a pilgrimage towards an understanding of the obvious in a world where the obvious is ignored. In her relations with three men she discovers the perennial optimist, the Officer, who never abandons his faith that Victoria will one day appear;

INTRODUCTION

the Lawyer, whose only remedy is to return to the past and its endless repetitions; and, finally, the Poet, in whom some glimmerings of understanding can be found. With understanding comes compassion. It is true that towards the end of the journey the Daughter can cry out, "You are all evil, evil!"; it is also true that from the beginning she repeats the untranslatable line "Det är synd om människorna": at times meaning little more than "what a shame about people," at times meaning "men are to be pitied," and at times carrying an emotive range whose only proper equivalent in English is perhaps "Father, forgive them, they know not what they do."

That the play is pessimistic seems beyond question. Although many of its ideas were familiar to Strindberg as a young man, they had been deepened by his reading, and perhaps most of all by his reading of Schopenhauer. In a passage from The World as Will and Idea, Schopenhauer expresses the basic message which Strindberg conveys:

> Awakened to life out of the night of unconsciousness, the will finds itself an individual, in an endless and boundless world, among innumerable individuals, all striving, suffering, erring; and as if through a troubled dream it hurries back to its old unconsciousness. Yet till then its desires are limitless, its claims inexhaustible, and every satisfied desire gives rise to a new one... Then let one consider what as a rule are the satisfactions of any kind that a man obtains. For the most part nothing more than the bare maintenance of his existence itself. ... Everything in life shows that earthly happiness is destined to be frustrated or shown to be an illusion... Life presents itself as a continual deception in small things as in great. If it has promised, it does not keep its word, unless to show how little worth desiring were the things desired; and thus we are deluded now by hope, now by what we hoped for... The enchantment of distance shows us paradises which vanish like optical illusions when we allow ourselves to be mocked by them. Happiness, accordingly, always lies in the future or in the past.

The Billsticker's line on attaining his fishnet and box after waiting for them for fifty years, "It's not exactly what I had in mind," could not more succinctly restate Schopenhauer's idea. Except, perhaps, that Strindberg was not certain that unconsciousness is our destination. He writes to Harriet Bosse in 1905:

> I struggle upwards, and yet sink down; I want what is right, and yet act wrongly; my old self is in conflict with my new; I want to see life as beautiful, yet only nature is beautiful; I have compassion for men but I cannot respect them, cannot love them, for I know them through myself. My only comfort is from

Buddha, who tells me plainly that life is a phantasm,
an illusion, which we will come to see properly in
another life. My hope and my future lie on the other
side; that is why I find life so hard to bear.

A Dream Play dramatizes the Daughter's awakening to this knowledge,
through a series of movements towards the illusory enchantments of
distance, whether the distance be one of concepts--"Love conquers
everything"--or of place, as in the ill-starred journeys to Foulstrand
and Fairhaven. Finally the Daughter's wandering spirit discovers
that this world means nothing, and, unlike the Deans of the Four
Faculties, she is content to accept that knowledge without needing
to systematize it or explain it. She recognizes the constant battle
between carnal reality and spiritual aspiration, and sees that in
the suffering which that battle causes lies man's only hope of expia-
tion and redemption. "The world, men, life itself, are merely a
phantasm, an illusion, a dream... Suffering became the source of
redemption."

For a drama this seems a ponderous theme, and sometimes A Dream
Play has been a ponderous experience. It should not be. Though its
import is pessimistic, its medium is comic. "Lord what fools these
mortals be" may be truth, but it is not tragedy, and A Dream Play
should be performed in the same spirit. The absurdist elements of
the schoolroom scene, as the Officer sadly attempts to reconcile age
with immaturity, and mathematics with logic, are the material for
laughter, not for tears. The Billsticker is not tragic. Nor is
the Quarantine Master's response as He and She step ashore to begin
their forty-day purgatory:

    HE   What have we done?
    Q.M. Done? You don't have to do anything to meet
    with life's little misfortunes!

There is both humor and pathos in Strindberg's decision to ensure
that none of the aspirations of his earthly characters is either important or attainable. Similarly none of the characters act with
purpose or understanding. They assume the validity of past and future,
even though the Officer is confronted at the play's opening with the
past still present before his eyes, and even though the future brings
nothing but a repetition of the past. They look for meaning where
there is no meaning to be found, but they do so in the spirit revealed
by the Officer as he pokes at the Lawyer's filing cabinet, unable to
understand why it is, and yet is not, the cloverleaf door of his own
theater alley. For all except the Daughter and the Poet, the play is
a cycle, bringing them once more to the point at which they started.
For the Daughter it is an escape from the cycle into the flames of
purgation and fruition; and for the Poet it is an approach to understanding of his dream.

MISS JULIE

FOREWORD

The theater has long seemed to me to be a Biblia pauperum, a Bible in pictures for those who cannot read, and I see the playwright as a lay preacher hawking modern ideas in a form popular enough for the middle classes, the mainstay of our audience, to understand without troubling their heads too much. The theater has always been an elementary school for the young, the half-educated, and for women-- those who retain the primitive capacity for self-deception and allow themselves to be deceived through the author's powers of suggestion. Today, when that rudimentary, immature mode of thinking expressed in fantasy is developing into reflection, investigation, and analysis, the theater may, like religion, be discarded as a dying form because we lack the prerequisites for appreciation. This view would appear to be supported by the prevailing theatrical crisis throughout Europe, not least in those civilized countries which have produced the greatest thinkers of the past, England and Germany, where the theater, like the other fine arts, is dead.

Elsewhere, however, people have attempted to reshape the drama by incorporating new ideas into the old dramatic forms. But the new ideas have not been popularized enough for audiences to grasp them easily, and sometimes strong opinions about them have heated their brains too much for any just appreciation. One cannot appreciate a play which contradicts one's innermost convictions, nor enjoy it when an applauding or a hissing audience expresses its opinions as openly as is possible in a public theater. It is also true that new content has rarely been accompanied by new forms, and the new wine has burst the ancient bottles.

In this play I have not tried to do anything new--that is impossible--but I have tried to modernize the form to meet the demands of modern men. To that end I have chosen--or been chosen by--a theme which can be said to lie outside the clash of contemporary opinion. The distinctions between rising or falling social classes, higher or lower, better or worse, man or woman, are, have always been, and always will be of abiding interest. When, a few years ago, I heard of this real-life incident, it made a powerful impression on me. I believed it suitable for tragedy because the extinction of a favored individual, and still more of a favored race, still appeals to the tragic sense. Perhaps we shall reach an enlightened stage of development in which the cruel and cynical drama of life will be a matter of indifference. Those mechanical responses called feelings may be superfluous and harmful to us when viewed with a more highly developed judgment, and we will dispense with them. The heroine only arouses our pity because we are frail enough to fear that her fate might overtake us. The highly sensitive spectator may find even this pity inadequate, while the optimist may demand some positive program for the remedy of evil. But there is no such thing as absolute evil, for even as one race is defeated another cheerfully takes its place; and then our satisfaction lies in comparing the rise and fall, since comparison is one of life's greatest pleasures. And to the optimist who would remedy the melancholy fact that the eagle preys on the dove, and the louse devours the eagle, I would ask: Why should it be remedied? Life is not so mathematically idiotic that only the great eat the small; it happens just as often that the bee kills the lion, or at least drives him mad.

If my play has a depressing effect on many of its spectators, it is their own fault. When we are as strong as the first revolutionaries in France, we will watch with ease and pleasure as the national parks are stripped of dark and ancient trees which have stood too long, to be replaced by others with an equal right to vegetate for their term. It is the kind of satisfaction one derives from the death of a terminally sick patient.

People complained recently that my tragedy The Father was too sad, as if they wanted cheerful tragedies. They call pretentiously for joie de vivre, and theater managers send out demands for farce, as if the joy of life lay in the stupidity of describing human beings as victims of St. Vitus's dance or idiocy. I find the joys of life in its hard, cruel struggles, and my pleasures lie in knowledge and discovery. And so I have chosen an unusual, but instructive, theme--in a word, an exception which proves the rule--which will, of course, offend all those who love the commonplace. That neither motivation nor point of view is simple will also offend the commonplace mind. But life's events--and this is a rather new discovery!--stem from a series of more or less obscure motives, and as a rule the observer merely chooses the most intelligible or the most creditable. Someone commits suicide. "Failure in business!" says the man of affairs. "Despised love!" say the women. "Terminal disease!" says the sick man. "Ruined hopes!" say the down-and-out. But probably the real motives lay somewhere else, or nowhere, or the dead man concealed his truest reasons beneath those which do more credit to his memory.

Miss Julie's lamentable fate is derived from a multitude of causes: her mother's basic instincts, her father's inappropriate teaching, her own nature and the influence of her fiancé on her weak, degenerate mind; and, more pertinently, the festive atmosphere of Midsummer's Eve, her father's absence, her monthly period, her contact with animals, the inflaming influence of the dance, the cover of night, the strongly aphrodisiac influence of the flowers, and, finally, chance, which confronts her with the enterprise of an aroused man and an enticing room.

Thus I have not ascribed a uniformly physiological or psychological cause. It is not simply the mother's inherited passion, the effects of menstruation, or "indecency." I have not even preached a moral! For lack of a priest, I have left that to the cook.

For this multiplicity of motive I can congratulate myself for being in harmony with the times! And if others have done the same before me I can congratulate myself in that I am not alone in my paradoxes, as all discoveries are called.

So far as characterization is concerned, I have made my figures rather "characterless," and for good reason.

In the course of time the word "character" has acquired a multiple significance. Probably it originally signified the dominant feature of the personality-complex, and was a synonym for "temperament." But later on it became a middle-class expression for an automaton. Anyone whose personality was static, or who adapted himself once and for all to a certain role in life--in other words anyone who ceased to grow--was called a character. Anyone whose personality developed, the skillful navigator on the stream of life, traveling not with sails fixed but veering and luffing in the wind, was said to lack character. It was a condemnation, of course, since he was so hard to capture, tabulate, or control. The middle-class concept of the immobility of personality was transported to the stage, where the middle class has always reigned supreme. The character became a man whose personality was conclusively fixed: always drunk, jocular, or wretched; needing only a physical defect--a club foot, a wooden leg, a red nose--or the repetition of a single verbal formula: "That's capital!," "Barkis is willing!," or the like. This naive view of mankind survives even in the great Moliere. Harpagon is merely avaricious, yet he could have remained avaricious and still have been an expert financier, a good father, a model citizen. To make matters worse, his "vice" is to the direct advantage of his son-in-law and daughter, since they are his heirs. They ought not to blame him, even if they have to wait awhile to get to bed together. I do not believe in such simple theatrical types. We should challenge an author's summary judgments of men: this one is stupid, this one brutal, this one stingy, and so on. And the Naturalists, who know how rich the soul-complex is, feel that "vice" has a reverse side which closely resembles virtue.

I have portrayed my characters, living as they do in a period of transition more vehemently hysterical than at least its predecessor, as unsettled, torn, a blend of the old and the new. And I have not thought it an improbability for modern ideas to seep down into the **servants'** quarters through the influence of newspapers and gossip.

My souls (characters) are conglomerates of bygone stages of civilization and progress, bits of books and newspapers, fragments of other people, torn-off rags from worn-out suits, patched together **just** as the personality is **patched** together. I have even given a little evolutionary history, since I allow the weaker to steal and repeat words from the stronger. We call this transference of ideas suggestion.

Miss Julie is a modern character, not because the half-woman, the man-hater, would not have been found at all times, but because she has now been recognized, has pushed herself forward and made a fuss. The half-woman is a self-assertive type, who sells herself for power, decorations, distinctions, and diplomas, just as she once sold herself for money, and she betrays her primitive origin. Hers is not a sound species, for it has no endurance, but it can still propagate its wretchedness: the degenerate man seems unconsciously to make his selection from it. Their offspring are of undecided sex, tortured by life. Fortunately they are destroyed, either by a lack of harmony with reality, the unchecked eruption of suppressed instincts, or failure to obtain a man. The type is tragic, offering as it does the drama of a confused struggle against nature, but it is a relic of romanticism now being dispersed by the Naturalists, who wish for nothing but happiness--and happiness demands a stronger and a better species.

But Miss Julie is also a relic of the old warrior aristocracy, now being replaced by the aristocracy of nerves and brain; a victim of the domestic conflict caused by her mother's "crime," a victim of the deluded thinking of the times, of circumstances, of her own defective constitution, all of which combine to form the equivalent of what was once called fate or universal law. The Naturalists abolished guilt when they abolished God; but they cannot abolish consequences, punishments, imprisonment, or fear, simply because they exist. Whether a man is acquitted or not, injured fellow citizens are not so obliging as unharmed outsiders can afford to be. Even if the father were compelled to forgo his revenge, the daughter would be avenged upon herself, as she is here, through that inborn or acquired sense of honor which the aristocracy inherits--from where? Whether from barbarian ancestors, primitive Aryans, or medieval chivalry, it does not lack beauty, but it is no longer effective for ensuring the survival of the race. It is the nobleman's hara-kiri, the inner scruples of the Japanese, leading them to slit open their own stomachs when their honor is affronted; and it survives in modified form in the aristocratic privilege of dueling. But though Julie cannot live on in dishonor, the retainer Jean survives.

It is the bondsman's advantage over the nobleman that he lacks this fatal principle of honor. Yet in all Aryans there is enough of the nobleman, or of Don Quixote, to prompt us to sympathy with the suicide who has lost his honor through his deeds. We suffer at the sight of fallen greatness littering the earth like a corpse, even if it should rise up and offer honorable compensation through new deeds. But the servant Jean is a race-builder whose uniqueness can be seen. The laborer's child has cultivated in himself the future gentleman. He has quick abilities, finely developed senses (smell, taste, and sight), even a sense of beauty. He has already risen in the world, and he is not too nice to exploit the services of others. To his comrades he is already alien, and he despises them as outgrown relics of his own past. But he fears them, too, and tries to escape from their knowledge of his secrets, their awareness of his plans, their envy of his success, and their complacent prediction of his downfall. This is the source of the duality of his uncompleted character, wavering between fellow feeling and hatred for the upper classes. As he says himself, he is an aristocrat, and he has learned the secrets of polite manners; but beneath his polish there is crudeness: although he wears his evening dress with taste, there is no guarantee that he has washed.

He respects Miss Julie, but he fears Kristin as the sharer of dangerous secrets. He is callous enough not to let the night's events interfere with his future plans. With the cruelty of the slave and the insensitivity of the master, he can look on blood without a tremor. He can accept misfortune and take it in his stride. He survives this conflict without injury, and no doubt he does become the proprietor of a hotel. And if he does not become a Rumanian count, no doubt his son will take a degree and end up as an attorney.

Moreover he offers some important insights into the lower-class view of life from below--when he speaks the truth, at least, which is not often the case. Words are more often framed for his advantage than for truth. When Miss Julie supposes that all the lower classes feel their oppression to be burdensome, he agrees as a matter of course, since his aim is to win her sympathy. But he changes his tune at once when it is to his advantage to distinguish himself from the mob.

Quite apart from his success as a social climber, Jean is superior to Miss Julie because he is a man. Sexually he is an aristocrat, through his masculine strength, his more finely developed senses, and his initiative. His inferiority lies chiefly in a temporary social setting, which he can probably lay aside with his servant's livery.

His inborn servility is expressed in his reverence for the Count (his boots), and in his religious superstition. But his reverence for the Count is little more than reverence for a status which he seeks to win for himself, and it does not survive his conquest of the daughter, when he has seen how empty is that beautiful shell.

I do not believe that love, in its "higher" sense, can arise between two such diverse characters, and I have made Julie imagine her love as a defense or an excuse, while Jean perceives clearly that his love for her would cease in other social circumstances. No doubt it is much the same with love as it is with hyacinths, which must put down roots in darkness before they can send up a strong bloom. Here it shoots up, blossoms, and germinates all at once, and so the plant dies quickly.

Kristin is a female slave, dependent on others, lethargic from her years before a kitchen stove, and crammed full with morality and religion, which she uses as a cloak and a scapegoat. She goes thoughtlessly to church to unload her household thefts onto Jesus, and to acquire a new pretense of innocence. She is a minor character, and deliberately sketched as such, as was the case with the pastor and the doctor in The Father, who are more or less typical of provincial priests and doctors. Some people have seen these minor sketches as abstractions, but that is because such people are abstract in their work. They are unoriginal, and in the conduct of their duties they show no more than one side of their being. So long as the spectators do not need to see them from several sides, my abstract sketches will do well enough.

To some extent, the dialogue is a break with tradition. I have not made my characters catechists, simply asking stupid questions to elicit smart replies. I have avoided the mathematical symmetry of French dialogue, and allowed their minds to work irregularly, as they do in life. A conversation does not exhaust its subject, and one mind provides the cog in which the other engages more or less at random. The dialogue wanders, for the same reason, providing material in early scenes which is later taken up, revised, repeated, expanded, and developed like a musical theme.

The plot is clear enough, and as it really deals with only two characters I have concentrated on them. There is only one extra person, the cook, though behind and over everything hovers the father's unhappy spirit. Most people today, I believe, take their greatest pleasure from the psychological process, and our inquiring spirits are not content simply with seeing an event take place; we want to know how it works. We want to see the puppet-strings, the machinery, explore the false-bottomed box, find the joint in the magician's ring, look at the cards to see how they are marked. In this I have had in mind the realistic novels of the Goncourt brothers, which have appealed to me more than any other contemporary literature.

I have abandoned the division into acts, as an experiment. It seemed to me that our declining capacity for illusion might be disturbed by an intermission during which the audience has time to think, and the author-hypnotist loses his suggestive influence. My play probably lasts for an hour and a half: when one can listen to a lecture, a sermon, or a conference address for as long or longer, I fancy that a ninety-minute drama is not too much. Back in 1872, in one of my first attempts at drama, The Outlaw, I tried this concentrated form, though with little success. I had written and completed a play in five acts, and I could see their unhappy, fragmenting influence. The play was burned, but from its ashes arose a single, thorough act of fifty printed pages, playing for about an hour. The form is not altogether new, but it seems to be my province, and perhaps, with changing laws of taste, it will become the future norm. I would hope to find a public educated enough to sit through a whole evening of a single act, but this needs experimentation first. For the moment, to provide respite for the audience and the actors without releasing them from the illusion, I have used three techniques, all of them dramatic: monologue, mime, and ballet. Originally they come from classical tragedy, the monody developing into the monologue, and the chorus into ballet. Monologue is sometimes condemned by our realists as improbable, but if properly motivated it seems probable enough to me, and I believe it can be used to advantage. For example, it is natural for an orator to pace up and down reciting his speech, for an actor to rehearse his role aloud, for a maidservant to gossip with the cat, a mother to prattle with her child, an old woman to jabber with her parrot, or for people to talk in their sleep. To offer the actor an occasional chance of independent work, free from the direction of the author, it is best simply to hint at a monologue rather than to prescribe a speech. Moreover, it is obviously immaterial what is said to a parrot, or in one's sleep, since it has no influence on the plot; and a gifted actor, confident of the atmosphere and the situation, can probably improvise this better than the author, who cannot foretell how much needs to be said, nor for how long, before the audience is awakened from its illusion.

As is well known, some Italian theaters have returned to improvisation, and produced creative actors, though in tune with the author's plans. This could be a step towards a new development of the art, and it is certainly productive.

Where monologue would be inappropriate, I have introduced mime, and have left the actor even more independence to create for himself, and win honor for himself. But in order not to strain the audience too much, I have had recourse to music--justified by the midsummer dance--and let it exercise its powers of suggestion and illusion. I would beg the director of music to take the selection of pieces much to heart; no alien atmosphere should be evoked, through reminiscences of popular operettas of the day, contemporary dance repertoires, or obvious and identifiable folk music.

I have introduced ballet as an alternative to the conventional "crowd" scenes, which are always played badly, and always contain a few feeble spirits who take their chance to be clever, and spoil the illusion. And as peasants do not improvise their abuse, but use material ready to hand and capable of double meanings, I have not written an original song, but have taken the words of a lesser-known dance which I transcribed in the neighborhood of Stockholm. The words apply approximately, though not exactly, to the situation; but that is deliberate, for weak, cowardly slaves will not permit themselves a direct attack. In a serious action, I have also excluded clowns: there can be no cheap sneers over a situation which lowers the lid on the coffin of a race.

I have borrowed my scenery from the Impressionists: the asymmetrical, and "partial" view. One does not see an entire room and furnishings, and is impelled to guess. In other words, the imagination is set in motion to complete the illusion. I have also taken pains to avoid tedious entrances and exits through doors: theater doors are made of cloth, and sway at the slightest movement. They lack even the capacity to lend expression to an incensed father's rage as he walks out after a poor dinner, slamming the door "so that the whole house trembles." In the theater it merely sways. I have also kept to a single set, both to allow the characters to grow into their milieu, and also to dispense with lavish scenery. When one has only one set one can also insist that it be more realistic. There is nothing more difficult to get than a room that looks like a room, however well the artist can paint volcanoes and waterfalls. But granted that the walls are made of cloth, do we have to accept painted bookcases and pots and pans? The stage relies on so many conventions already that I believe we could dispense with painted saucepans.

With the rear wall and table at an angle, the actors can face one another across the table, and play full face and profile. In the opera Aida, I have seen an angled table which led out to unknown perspectives, and I had no sense it was done merely in reaction against boring straight lines.

Another necessary innovation is the removal of the footlights. These have the effect of making the actor look fatter in the face. But why should they? Moreover the footlights erase a number of features, especially in the lower part of the face. The chin disappears, the nose is distorted, and it casts a shadow on the actors' eyes. Even if this were not true, it is true that the full play of the eyes is lost. The glare of footlights hits the retina on a normally sheltered spot (though it is the same for sailors who see the sun reflected off the water), and so one seldom sees an eye gesture except crude stares into the wings or up into the gallery. Actresses in particular often blink continually from the same cause. And when anyone on the stage wishes to speak with his eyes, he can only stare directly at the audience, bringing himself into immediate contact with them. From this habit arises the bad practice of what is often called "greeting one's friends."

Surely a sufficiently strong sidelight (with some kind of reflectors) would offer the actor this new resource: to perform with one of the strongest assets of the face: the eyes?

I have few illusions that I can persuade actors to perform for the audience rather than with them, however desirable this might be. It is beyond my dreams that I will ever see the actor's back throughout an important scene; but I do wish that decisive scenes could be played on the spot required by the situation, and not directly in front of the prompt box, like partners in a duel waiting for applause. You see, I am not suggesting a revolution; only small modifications. To have a scene in a room whose fourth wall is missing, and to actually see the back of some of the furniture, would really disturb the audience!

When I speak of makeup, I dare not hope to be listened to by the ladies, who would rather be beautiful than probable. But the actor might consider whether it is to his advantage to paint onto his face an abstract character who will sit there like a mask. Consider the man who draws in charcoal a choleric line between the eyes, and then, with this permanent feature engraved on him, must smile in response to a line. What kind of terrible grimace would he produce? And how will that brow smooth as a billiard ball wrinkle when the old man is angry?

In a modern psychological drama, where the soul's most delicate motions should be reflected more in the face than in words or gestures, it would be best to experiment with a small stage in a small auditorium, with bright sidelights and little or no makeup.

We should also dispense with the visible orchestra, with its distracting lights, and its faces gazing at the audience. If we could get rid of the boxes, too, we could **dispense** with chattering diners and their parties, and have complete darkness in the auditorium. And if, most of all, we could have a <u>small</u> stage and a <u>small</u> auditorium, then perhaps a new drama would arise, and the theater would once more be a place for the entertainment of educated men. While waiting for such a theater, we can write the laws and prepare the repertoire which must come.

I have made an attempt! If it has failed, there is time to try again!

(A large kitchen whose walls and ceiling are concealed by draperies. The rear wall runs diagonally inwards and upwards from the left. Against it are two sets of shelves containing china, **pewter, pots and** pans, etc. The shelves are decorated with scalloped paper. Further to the right we see three-quarters of the large vaulted exit, with two glass doors through which can be seen a fountain in the form of a Cupid, lilac bushes in full bloom, and poplar trees.

To the left is the corner of a large kitchen stove and part of the chimney. To the right, one end of the servants' table and a few chairs.

The stove is decorated with birch branches, and the floor with juniper, in honor of Midsummer's Eve.

A large Japanese spice box stands on the table, near a vase of lilacs. Nearby are an icebox, a side table, and a kitchen sink. Above the door is a large old-fashioned bell, and on the left a speaking tube.

KRISTIN stands at the stove, dressed in light woolens and an apron. JEAN enters, dressed in servant's livery, and carrying a large pair of spurred riding boots which he places conspicuously on the floor.

JEAN Miss Julie is crazy this evening, just crazy!

KRISTIN Well, here you are!

JEAN I went to the station with the Count. When I came back I dropped by the barn for a dance, and there was Miss Julie dancing with the gamekeeper! As soon as she saw me, she rushed straight over and offered me the ladies' waltz--and when she waltzed! I've never seen anything like it! She's crazy!

KRISTIN She's always been crazy, and for the last few weeks she's been worse--ever since she broke off her engagement.

JEAN Yes. What was that all about, anyway? He was a pretty good fellow, even if he wasn't rich. But they're all so damned choosy. (Sits at the end of the table.) Why is she staying here tonight, instead of going with her father to their cousins'?

KRISTIN After that fiasco of an engagement she daren't show her face.

JEAN Could be. Still, he could stand up for himself. Do you know what happened? I saw it--though I wasn't going to say so.

KRISTIN You saw it?

JEAN Yes. They were out by the stables one night, and she was "training" him, as she calls it. You know what she did? She made him jump over her riding crop like a dog! He did it twice, and both times she hit him with the crop. The third time he snatched it out of her hand and broke it to bits. Then he took off.

MISS JULIE

KRISTIN She did that! I can't believe it!

JEAN Well, that's what happened. What have you got for me, Kristin?

KRISTIN Just a small kidney. I cut it out of their veal.

JEAN Delicious! My great délice! But you might have warmed the plate.

KRISTIN (pulling his hair affectionately) You're fussier than the Count himself when you've a mind to be.

JEAN Don't pull me about! You know how sensitive I am.

KRISTIN Well, it's only for love.

(JEAN eats. KRISTIN opens a bottle of beer.)

JEAN Beer! On Midsummer Eve! No thanks, I have something better than that.

(He takes a bottle of red wine from the cupboard.)

Look at that! Gold seal! Give me a glass--a wine glass! I'm drinking this straight.

KRISTIN Lord help anyone who gets you for a husband. Always a fuss!

JEAN Nonsense! You'd be glad to have a man like me. And I don't see your reputation getting hurt when people say I'm your fiancé! (Samples the wine.) Good! Really good! But not quite room temperature! (Warms the glass in his hands.) Bought in Dijon, at four francs a liter, not counting the bottle! And then there was the tax! What foul-smelling brew are you cooking now?

KRISTIN Oh, its just some shit Miss Julie wants for Diana.

JEAN Kristin, watch your tongue! How can you stand there cooking dog's meat on a holiday? Is the bitch sick?

KRISTIN Sick enough! She's been sneaking round the gatekeeper's pug again--you know what that means. And Miss Julie won't hear of it!

JEAN Sometimes she's so high-and-mighty--and sometimes she hasn't any pride at all. Just like her mother when she was alive. She felt most at home in the kitchen or the barn, but did you ever see her drive with less than two horses? Went around with dirty cuffs--and the family coat-of-arms on her cuff links! As for Miss Julie--she's got no respect for her place. I could say she isn't refined. Just now, when I was dancing in the barn, she took the gamekeeper away from Anna and kept him to herself. You'd never catch one of us doing that. But it's always the same when they want to join in with us-- they're just cheap!--But she is handsome! Splendid! What shoulders!

What...etc.!

KRISTIN   That's what you say! Clara helps her to dress, and I've heard what she says too!

JEAN   Clara! You're all jealous of one another. I've been riding with her--and you should see her dance!

KRISTIN   Jean, will you dance with me when I'm through?

JEAN   Yes, of course I will.

KRISTIN   Is that a promise?

JEAN   Promise? When I say I'll do a thing, I'll do it. Thanks for the meal. Delicious!

(He replaces the cork in the bottle. MISS JULIE enters, still talking to people outside.)

JULIE   Don't wait for me. I'll be right back.

(JEAN hides the bottle in a drawer, and rises respectfully. JULIE goes straight to KRISTIN.)

JULIE   Is everything ready?

JEAN (gallant)   Do you two ladies have secrets?

JULIE (slapping his face with her handkerchief)   Curious?

JEAN   Oh how that smells of violets!

JULIE (coquettish)   Insolence! Are you an expert on perfumes too? Still, you dance well enough. Now, don't look. Just go.

JEAN (mock-polite)   Is this some witches' brew the ladies concoct each midsummer night? Some way of telling the stars or foreseeing the future?

JULIE (sharply)   If you can see that you have sharp eyes! (To KRISTIN.) Put it in a bottle and cork it. Jean, come and dance the schottische with me!

JEAN (hesitating)   I don't want to seem rude, but I'd promised this dance to Kristin...

JULIE   Well, she can have one later! Isn't that right, Kristin? You'll lend Jean to me, won't you?

KRISTIN   It's not up to me. (To JEAN.) If Miss Julie does you the honor, it's not right to say no. Go on; you should be grateful.

JEAN To tell the truth, I don't want to hurt anyone's feelings... Is it wise for Miss Julie to dance twice in a row with the same man? The way these people talk...

JULIE What? What kind of talk? What do you mean?

JEAN If you won't understand, I'll speak more plainly. It looks bad to prefer one of your servants when there are others waiting for the same honor.

JULIE Prefer? What an idea! You astonish me. I am the mistress of this house, and if I honor you people with my presence and want to dance, I expect to dance with someone who knows how to lead. I don't want to make a fool of myself!

JEAN As you wish. I am at your service.

JULIE (gently) Don't take it as an order. This evening we're all equal, just happy people enjoying ourselves. So, give me your arm. Don't worry, Kristin, I shan't steal your fiancé.

(JEAN offers her his arm and leads her away. KRISTIN is left alone. In the distance we can hear faintly the violins playing a schottische. KRISTIN hums to the music, clears the table, washes the dishes, and places them in the cupboard. She takes off her apron, takes a mirror from the table drawer, and props it against the vase of lilac on the table. She lights a candle, warms a hairpin in its flame, and curls the hair above her forehead. For a while she stands by the door, listening, then returns to the table. She finds Julie's handkerchief, sniffs it, then folds it in four and smooths it.

This should be played as if the actress were alone in the theater. When need be, she turns her back to the audience. She never looks at them, and should not acknowledge their presence by hastening her actions. There should be no hurry whatever in her movements.

JEAN enters alone.)

JEAN I told you she's crazy! What a way to dance! People were jeering at her behind the doors. What do you think of that, Kristin?

KRISTIN Well, it's the time of the month. She's always strange then. Are you coming to dance with me now?

JEAN You're not angry with me for standing you up...?

KRISTIN No! Not for a little thing like that, you know very well. Besides I know my place.

JEAN (laying a hand on her breast) You're a sensible woman, Kristin, you'll make a good wife.

JULIE (enters, unpleasantly surprised) What a charming escort--running away from your partner!

JEAN Not at all, Miss Julie. As you see, I've rushed back to the one I deserted!

JULIE I've never known anyone dance so well! But why are you wearing your livery on a holiday? Take it off at once!

JEAN Then you must excuse me for a moment. My coat is in here...

JULIE Do I embarrass you? Just to change a coat? Go on then, but be quick. I could turn my back, you know!

JEAN With your permission...

(He exits right. We see his arm as he changes his coat.)

JULIE He's so discreet, Kristin! Is he your fiancé?

KRISTIN Fiancé? Yes, if you like. That's what we call it.

JULIE That's what you call it?

KRISTIN Yes. You've been engaged...

JULIE But we were really engaged!

KRISTIN It still didn't come to anything, did it...

(JEAN returns in a black evening coat and hat.)

JULIE Très gentil, Monsieur Jean, très gentil.

JEAN Vous voulez plaisanter, madame!

JULIE Et vous parler francais! Where did you learn?

JEAN Switzerland. I was the butler at the biggest hotel in Lucerne.

JULIE And you look quite the gentleman in that coat. Charmant!

JEAN You're flattering me.

JULIE Flattering you?

JEAN My natural modesty forbids me to believe that you would say such things to me truthfully; allow me to believe that you exaggerate--flattery!

JULIE Where did you learn to speak like that? You must have been to the theater!

MISS JULIE

JEAN   Just so. I have been many places.

JULIE Where were you born?

JEAN   My father worked for the public attorney. I knew you as a child; though you didn't know me.

JULIE No, really!

JEAN   Yes. I remember once...but I'd better not mention that!

JULIE Oh, tell me! What was it? Please tell me.

JEAN   No, not now, really. Another time perhaps.

JULIE Another time? That's an evasion. Is it so dangerous to tell me now?

JEAN   Dangerous, no--but it wouldn't be right. Look at her!

(KRISTIN has fallen asleep.)

JULIE She'll make a nice wife, I must say! She probably snores too.

JEAN   No she doesn't; but she does talk in her sleep.

JULIE How do you know that?

JEAN   I've heard her.

(Pause, during which they stare at one another.)

JULIE Why don't you sit down?

JEAN   I couldn't do that in your presence.

JULIE And if I order you to?

JEAN   Then I will obey.

JULIE Sit down then! no, stop! Can you get me a drink first?

JEAN   I don't know what's in the icebox. I'm afraid it's nothing but beer.

JULIE Nothing but beer! I have simple tastes--I'd rather have beer than wine.

(JEAN takes a beer bottle from the icebox, fills a glass, and serves it on a plate.)

JULIE Thank you. Aren't you having any?

JEAN I'm not keen on it, unless you order me to have it.

JULIE Order? Don't you think it would be polite to keep your partner company?

JEAN Well, that's true enough.

(He opens another bottle and fills his glass.)

JULIE Now, drink my health! Why, I believe you're shy!

(JEAN falls on his knees in parody; raises his glass.)

JEAN To my mistress's health!

JULIE Bravo! Now you must kiss my foot, and everything will be perfect.

(JEAN hesitates for a moment, then boldly seizes her foot and kisses it.)

Excellent! You should have been an actor!

JEAN This must stop. Someone might come in and see us!

JULIE What does that matter?

JEAN People would talk, that's all. And if you knew what they were saying up there just now...

JULIE What were they saying? Tell me.--Sit down now!

JEAN I don't want to hurt your feelings--but the sort of language they were using--suggested that...oh, you can guess! You're not a child. When people see a woman drinking alone with a man--especially with one of her servants--in the middle of the night...then...

JULIE Then what? Anyway, we're not alone. Kristin is here.

JEAN Sleeping!

JULIE Then I'll wake her up. Kristin! Kristin, are you asleep?

(KRISTIN mumbles in her sleep.)

Kristin! How she can sleep!

KRISTIN I've done the Count's shoes. Put on the coffee...quickly... quickly!...

JULIE (holding KRISTIN'S nose) Will you wake up!

JEAN (sharply) Don't disturb her when she's sleeping!

JULIE What?

JEAN People who have stood by a stove all day can be tired by nightfall. You ought to respect her sleep.

JULIE What a beautiful idea! It does you credit. Thank you. (Stretching her hand to him.) Come and gather lilac with me.

(During the following scene KRISTIN walks sleepily out to go to bed.)

JEAN With you?

JULIE With me!

JEAN No, I can't! Absolutely not!

JULIE I don't understand you. Can you possibly imagine...

JEAN Not me! Other people!

JULIE What? That I'm in love with my servant?

JEAN I'm not a conceited man, but it's happened before. And nothing is sacred to these people.

JULIE I believe you're an aristocrat.

JEAN Yes; I am.

JULIE I come down...

JEAN Don't come down, Miss Julie! Take my advice. No one will believe you did it from choice. They'll say you fell.

JULIE I think better of them than you do. Come!

(She gazes into his eyes.)

JEAN You are so strange.

JULIE Perhaps. But so are you--everything is strange! Life, people, everything--scum blown along the water until it sinks. I remember a dream I have now and then: I'm sitting high up on a pillar, and I can't get down. Every time I look at the ground my head spins, and I have to get down, but I don't have the courage to jump. I can't hold on and I'm longing to fall, but I can't do it. I can get no peace before I come down, no rest before I come down, down to the ground. And if I reached the ground I would want to go on, sinking down, into the earth. Have you ever had a dream like that?

JEAN No. I dream that I am lying under a great tree in the middle of a dark forest. I want to get up, up to the top, and look out across the fair land, out into the sunshine. I want to rob the nest of its golden eggs. And then I'm climbing, climbing upwards, but the trunk is thick and smooth, and the first branch is so far away. I know that once I reach that branch it will be as easy as climbing a ladder. I've never got there yet. But I shall, if only in my dreams.

JULIE   Here I stand, talking about dreams! Come now! Just out into the grounds!

JEAN   We should sleep on nine midsummer flowers tonight; then our dreams would come true.

(As they reach the door he claps his hand to his eye.)

JULIE   Let me see what's in your eye.

JEAN   It's nothing. Just a speck. It'll go away.

JULIE   My sleeve must have caught your eye. Sit down while I help you.

(She takes his arm and leads him to a chair, holds his head back, and removes the dust with the corner of her handkerchief.)

Sit down now, quite still! Now will you obey me!--I believe you're trembling, a big strong boy like you. With such arms!

JEAN (warningly)   Miss Julie!

JULIE   Yes, Monsieur Jean?

JEAN   Attention! Je ne suis qu'un homme!

JULIE   Will you sit still!--There, all gone! Kiss my hand and thank me.

JEAN (rising)   Miss Julie, listen to me! Kristin has gone to bed. Will you listen!

JULIE   Kiss my hand first.

JEAN   Be careful!

JULIE   Of what?

JEAN   Are you a twenty-five-year-old child? Don't you know it's dangerous to play with fire?

JULIE   Not for me. I'm insured!

JEAN   No you are not! And even if you are, there's enough here to kindle a flame.

JULIE   Meaning you?

MISS JULIE

JEAN Meaning me. Not just because I'm me, but because I'm a young man...

JULIE And a handsome one! What incredible conceit! A Don Juan, perhaps? Or a Joseph? I do believe you are a Joseph!

JEAN You think so?

JULIE You almost frighten me!

(JEAN attempts to embrace her and kiss her. She boxes his ears.)

JEAN Was that a joke, or were you serious?

JULIE Serious!

JEAN Then you were also serious just now! You play your games much too seriously, and that's risky. But I'm tired of games. If you'll excuse me I'll return to my work. The Count wants his boots on time, and it's long past midnight.

JULIE Put those boots down!

JEAN No, it's my duty! I have to do them. But it's not my duty to play games with you, and never will be. I'm too good for that.

JULIE You're very proud!

JEAN Sometimes; not always.

JULIE Have you ever been in love?

JEAN We don't use that word. I've had plenty of girls, if that's what you mean. And once I was sick because I couldn't have the one I wanted. Just like the princes in the Arabian Nights! I was so in love I couldn't eat or drink.

JULIE Who was she?

(JEAN does not answer.)

Who was she?

JEAN You can't force me to tell you.

JULIE Then let me ask you as an equal, as a friend.

JEAN You.

JULIE (sitting) How precious!

JEAN If you like. It was stupid. That was the story I wouldn't tell you before. But it was like this: do you know how the world looks from down there? No, of course not. You're all like the hawks and falcons whose backs one never sees because they are always hovering above you. I lived in a cottage with seven children and a pig, out in the gray fields where even the trees won't grow. From our window we could see the manor wall, and we could see apple trees blossoming on the other side. It was the Garden of Eden, guarded by hosts of evil angels with flaming swords. Even so, I and some other boys found our way to the tree of life. And now you despise me?

JULIE   Oh, every little boy steals apples.

JEAN   You can say that, but you still despise me. Very well! One day I came into the garden with my mother to weed the onion beds. By the kitchen garden there was a Turkish pavilion in the shadows of the jasmine trees, completely grown over with hyacinths. I didn't know what it was for, but I'd never seen such a beautiful building. People went in and out, and one day one of them left the door open. I crept in and saw the walls hung with pictures of kings and emperors, and there were red curtains with tassels hanging from them--you know what I mean.

(He breaks off a lilac blossom and holds it beneath her nose.)

I had never been in a castle, though I had been in a church, but this was more beautiful; and wherever my thoughts took me they always brought me back here. Eventually I was filled with longing to feel that joy again--enfin, I crept in, and looked at it again in admiration. Then someone came. There was only one way in and out for the gentry, but there was another one for me, and I had to use it.

(JULIE, who has taken the lilac, lets it fall on the table.)

Then I ran, burst through the raspberry bushes, raced straight over the strawberry beds and came up to the rose terrace. And there I saw a pink dress and a pair of white stockings--it was you. I crawled under a pile of weeds, among prickly thistles and foul-smelling water. I watched you as you walked through the roses, and I thought to myself: if it's true that a thief can enter into the kingdom and be among angels, then it's strange that a poor child on God's earth cannot get into the manor garden and play with a Count's daughter.

JULIE (wistfully)   Do you think all poor children think the same thing?

JEAN (doubtful at first, then more confidently)   All poor children. Yes, of course--of course!

JULIE   It must be so wretched to be poor!

JEAN (with exaggerated emotion)   Oh, Miss Julie, oh!--a dog can lie on your sofa, a horse can be stroked by you--but a peasant!--I know, there is always someone, somewhere, who has the force to rise in the world, but how often does that happen?--Anyway, do you know what I did? I ran down into the millstream, fully clothed; they dragged me out, and I was beaten. But the next Sunday, when the others had gone to visit my grandmother, I managed to stay home. I washed in soap and hot water, put on my best clothes, and went to church so that I could see you there. I saw you. Then I went home, determined to die. But I wanted to die easily, without pain. I remembered it was dangerous to sleep under an elder bush. We had a large one in full bloom. I stripped it of every flower, and lay down in the oat bin with them. Did you ever notice how smooth oats are? Smooth as the human skin! Anyway, I pulled the lid down, and dozed off. I slept for a long time, and when I came to I was seriously ill. Still, as you can see, I didn't die. I don't know what I wanted. There was no hope of winning you; but you showed me how hopeless it was for a man ever to get out of the place to which he was born.

JULIE You tell a beautiful story! Did you ever go to school?

JEAN Not much. But I've read plenty of novels, and I've been to the theater. Besides, I've heard the gentry talk, and I learned most of it from them!

JULIE You stand around listening to what we say?

JEAN Of course! Sitting up on the box, or rowing the boat, I've heard plenty. Once I heard you and a lady friend...

JULIE Oh! What did you hear?

JEAN It won't bear repeating! But I admit I was surprised--I don't understand where you could learn such words. Perhaps when you get down to it, there isn't as much difference as we think between people.

JULIE What do you mean! We don't behave the way you do when we're engaged!

JEAN (staring into her eyes) Are you quite sure of that? You don't have to play the innocent for my sake...

JULIE I gave my love to a scoundrel...

JEAN That's what they always say--afterwards.

JULIE Always?

JEAN I think so. I've heard the phrase several times before in one place or another.

JULIE Where?

JEAN Situations like this one. The last time...

JULIE Silence! I don't want to hear about it!

JEAN Neither did she. Isn't that strange? Well, let me get to bed.

JULIE Bed, on Midsummer Night!

JEAN Yes, I really don't fancy dancing with that rabble up there.

JULIE Get the key to the boathouse, and row me out onto the lake. I want to see the sunrise!

JEAN Is that wise?

JULIE You sound as if you're afraid for your reputation!

JEAN Why not? I don't want to make a fool of myself, and I don't want to be thrown out without a reference. I want to be able to strike out on my own. Anyway, I've got a responsibility towards Kristin...

JULIE Oh, so it's Kristin now...

JEAN Yes, but it's you too. Take my advice, and go to bed.

JULIE Am I supposed to obey you?

JEAN Just for once, for your own sake! I beg you. The night's half-gone, and when we're sleepy we're drunk and hotheaded. Go to bed! Besides, if I'm hearing right, those people are on their way up here to fetch me. If they find us both we've had it.

(The crowd approaches, singing:)

> Two old women came out of the wood,
> Tridiridi-ralla, tridiridi-ra,
> One had her feet as wet as she could,
> Tridiridi-ralla-la.
>
> They talked of wealth beyond measure,
> Tridiridi-ralla, tridiridi-ra,
> But a farthing was their whole treasure,
> Tridiridi-ralla-la.
>
> Garlands I place on your brow,
> Tridiridi-ralla, tridiridi-ra,
> But I wish someone else had me now,
> Tridiridi-ralla-la.

JULIE I know these people, and I love them just as they love me. You'll see. Let them in.

JEAN No, Miss Julie, they do not love you! They take your bread and they spit on it. Believe me. Listen to them, listen to what they're singing--No, don't listen to them!

MISS JULIE 25

JULIE   What are they singing?

JEAN   Just a burlesque--about you and me.

JULIE   How dare they! The lying...

JEAN   The rabble are always cowards. But if you get into a fight with them, it's still better to run.

JULIE   Run? Where? We can't get out, and we can't go into Kristin's room...

JEAN   Then we'll have to go into mine. Necessity knows no law. You can trust me; I really am your honest and respectful friend.

JULIE   But what if they look for you there?

JEAN   I'll bolt the door. If anyone tries to get in then, I'll shoot!-- Come with me... (Kneeling.) Come!

JULIE   You promise?

JEAN   I swear!

(They exit right, hastily.

BALLET: The countrypeople in holiday dress and with flowers in their hats, a fiddler in the lead. They lay a keg of beer and a cask of brännvin on the table, and fill their glasses from them. As they drink they form a ring and dance to the tune of "Two old women." At the end of the dance they leave, still singing.

JULIE enters alone, and gazes at the devastated kitchen, wringing her hands. She takes out a powderpuff and powders her face.)

JEAN (triumphant)   There, you see? You heard them! Do you still think we can stay here?

JULIE   No, but what shall we do!

JEAN   Escape! Get away from here!

JULIE   Escape? Where to?

JEAN   Switzerland, the Italian lakes. Have you ever been?

JULIE   No, is it beautiful?

JEAN   An eternal summer! Oranges, laurel groves...

JULIE   Well, what do we do then?

JEAN   Start a hotel! First-class service for first-class customers!

JULIE   Hotel?

JEAN   That's the life, believe me. New faces all the time, new languages. Not a minute to spare for nerves or brooding, no sitting around wondering what to do--the work just comes rolling in: bells ringing night and day, trains whistling and buses coming and going, and all the time the cash is rolling in too. That's the life!

JULIE   But what would I do?

JEAN   Mistress of the household, and pride of the firm! With your looks and manners--we can't lose. You'd sit like a queen in the office, setting slaves in motion at the touch of a button. The guests would pass before your throne and humbly lay their treasure before you-- you can't believe how scared people get when they have to pay a bill. While I'm cooking the books, you'll be sweetening them up with your loveliest smile--oh, let's get out of here! (Picks up a railway timetable.) Quick! The next train! That brings us to Malmö at 6:30, Hamburg 8:40 tomorrow morning; one day from Frankfurt to Basel, and through the St. Gotthard to Como in, let's see, three days. Three days!

JULIE   That's all very well, but Jean--you must give me the strength. Tell me you love me. Kiss me!

JEAN (hesitating)   I would--but I daren't! Not again in this house. Of course I love you Miss Julie; can you doubt it?

JULIE (shy, very feminine)   Call me Julie! There mustn't be any distance between us now. Call me Julie!

JEAN   I can't! There is a distance between us, as long as we stay in this house! There's the past, there's the Count--and I never knew anyone I was so much afraid of. I feel insignificant if I just see his gloves lying in a chair! If I hear that bell up there I shy like a frightened horse; and look at those boots, standing there, stiff, arrogant--I feel my back beginning to bend at the very sight of them! (Kicks the boots away.) Superstition, out of date, and beaten into us as children!--But no more easily forgotten for all that. Just come to another country, a republic, where people will bow down before a servant's livery. Yes, they will bow down, but I shan't! I wasn't born to bow, I've got force, character, and as soon as I reach that first branch just watch me leap to the top of the tree! Today a servant--but next year a proprietor, in ten years a landowner--and then, I think, I'll travel to Rumania, let them decorate me, and perhaps-- only perhaps, notice--I may end up as a count!

JULIE   Wonderful, wonderful!

JEAN   Well, in Rumania I could buy the title--and then you'll be a countess. My countess!

JULIE   Why should I care! I'm leaving all that behind me. Tell

MISS JULIE

you love me...because...because...otherwise, what am I?

JEAN I'll tell you a thousand times--later! But not here! We'll lose everything if we get sentimental now. Let's keep our heads, like sensible people. (Trims and lights a cigar.) Now, you sit there, I'll sit here, and we'll talk as if nothing has happened.

JULIE Oh my God, have you no feelings?

JEAN Feelings! There's not a man alive more sensitive than I am. But I can control myself.

JULIE A little while ago you could kiss my foot--and now!

JEAN Yes--a little while ago! Now we've got other things to think about.

JULIE Don't speak so roughly.

JEAN Not roughly; sensibly! We've made fools of ourselves once, don't let's do it again. The Count could be here at any moment, and we'd better plan our fate before he comes. Now, what do you think of my plans? Do you like them?

JULIE They seem good enough to me--but what about capital? Do you have any?

JEAN Me? Of course! My abilities, my boundless experience, my mastery of foreign languages! That's capital enough, if you ask me.

JULIE But it won't even buy you a railway ticket!

JEAN True enough. That's why I need a partner to provide funds.

JULIE Where are you going to get him at this time of night?

JEAN Me? You're going to find him, if you want to come with me.

JULIE How can I do that? I don't have anything at all myself.

(Pause.)

JEAN Then we've had it!

JULIE And...

JEAN We stay here.

JULIE Do you think I can stay under this roof as your plaything? Do you think I'm going to put up with local gossip, or look my father in the face again, after this? No! I want to get out of here, away from humiliation and disgrace.--Oh what have I done, my God, what have I done!

JEAN Do you have to start that? What have you done? The same as plenty before you!

JULIE (hysterically) And you despise me!--I'm falling, I'm falling!

JEAN Fall down to me and I will raise you up again.

JULIE What awful power drew me to you? Weakness drawn by strength? The dying class attracted by the new? Or was it love? This love? Do you know what love is?

JEAN Yes, I promise you. Do you think I haven't been in love before?

JULIE What are you saying, what are you thinking?

JEAN I'm just what I've been taught. Now, don't be so neurotic and hysterical. We're both in the same boat now. There, there, little girl. Let's have another glass!

(Takes the wine bottle out of the drawer and fills two of the used glasses.)

JULIE Where did you get that wine?

JEAN Out of the cellar!

JULIE My father's burgundy!

JEAN It's good for the stomach!

JULIE And I usually drink beer!

JEAN It just shows--you've got worse taste than I have.

JULIE Thief!

JEAN Do you want a fight?

JULIE Oh, oh! Accomplice to a petty thief! Was I drunk, or walking in my sleep? Midsummer Night! The feast of innocent games!

JEAN Innocent? Hm!

JULIE (walking to and fro) Is there anyone on earth as miserable as I am now!

JEAN Why? After such a conquest! Think of Kristin in there, don't you think she has feelings too?

JULIE I thought so once, but not now. A peasant is a peasant!

JEAN And a whore is a whore!

JULIE (on her knees, hands clasped)   God in heaven, make an end of my wretched life! Take me out of this filth! Save me, save me!

JEAN   I must say, it's painful to look at you. When I lay in the onion bed and watched you among the roses--I can tell you now--I had the same dirty thoughts as any other boy!

JULIE   You said you would die for me!

JEAN   In an oat bin? That was just a figure of speech.

JULIE   You mean lies!

JEAN (growing sleepy)   Near enough. I did read a story in a magazine once about a chimney sweep who shut himself into a box full of lilac because he'd been slapped with a paternity suit.

JULIE   What sort of man are you!

JEAN   What am I supposed to say? You've got to say something if you're trying to get a woman.

JULIE   Scoundrel!

JEAN   Merde!

JULIE   And now you've seen the falcon's back.

JEAN   Well, not exactly its back...

JULIE   And I was supposed to be the first branch.

JEAN   Yes, but the branch was rotten...

JULIE   To be displayed in a hotel...

JEAN   And the hotel...

JULIE   Sit at a counter, attract the guests, cook the books...

JEAN   No! I could do that myself!

JULIE   To think that a human soul can be so filthy!

JEAN   Wash it then!

JULIE   Lackey, servant, stand up when I speak to you!

JEAN   Lackey's slut, servant's whore, shut your mouth and get out of here! You say I'm crude! I've never seen any of my people behave as crudely as you did tonight. Do you think a serving wench would accost a man the way you did? Have you ever seen a girl in my class offer herself like you? The only place I've seen it is among animals and whores!

JULIE That's right, hit me, kick me, I don't deserve better. I'm a wretch, but help me! Help me to get out of here, if there is a way!

JEAN (gentler) I don't want to slander myself by declining the honor of having seduced you; but do you believe a man in my place would have dared raise his eyes to you if you yourself had not invited him? I'm still amazed...

JULIE And proud!

JEAN Why not? Though the victory was too easy to get very excited about it.

JULIE Hit me again!

JEAN No! Instead, forgive me for what I have said. I don't attack a disarmed enemy, least of all a woman. I won't deny that I'm glad to know that there's only a hairsbreadth of difference between us, to know that the hawk has a gray back too, that those elegant cheeks are powdered, that those polished nails are dirty, and that your handkerchief is dirty even though it smells of violets...on the other hand, it's painful to find out that what I am striving for is no higher or better than I am. It's painful to see you as you are now, sunk lower than the meanest kitchen wench--like seeing the autumn flowers whipped apart by the rain and trampled into the dirt.

JULIE You speak as if you were already superior to me.

JEAN I am. I could make you a countess, but you could never make me a count.

JULIE But I was born of a count. That you can never be!

JEAN True; but if my sons are counts...

JULIE You are a thief; I am not!

JEAN There are worse things than thieves. Besides, when I work in a house I see myself, to some extent at least, as a member of the family, almost like one of the children. And you don't call it theft when a child sneaks a berry from a full bush. (His ardor is growing again.) Miss Julie, you're a glorious woman, too good for the likes of me. You were carried away, and you're fooling yourself with the excuse that you love me. You don't--unless you were attracted by my looks, in which case your love is no better than mine; but I couldn't be happy to live simply as your lapdog; and I can never make you love me.

JULIE Are you sure of that?

JEAN You want to think it's possible! I would be able to love you, I know; you have beauty, elegance, (Takes her hand.) education, you're even lovable when you want to be. A man's passion for you could never be extinguished. (Lays his hand on her breast.) You're like wine, warm and full of spice, and a kiss from you...

(He tries to lead her out, but she slowly breaks loose.)

JULIE   Leave me alone!--You can't win me like that.

JEAN   Then how? Not like that? Not with caresses and fine words, plans for the future, rescue from humiliation? Then what should I do?

JULIE   I don't know, I don't know at all! I hate you as I hate rats--but I can't get away from you.

JEAN   Get away with me!

JULIE   I must! But I am so tired. Give me a glass of wine.

(JEAN pours the wine.)

We must talk first. We still have a little time left.

JEAN   Don't drink so fast. You'll be drunk.

JULIE   What does it matter?

JEAN   What does it matter? It's childish to get drunk. What do you want to talk about?

JULIE   Getting away! But I must talk first--so far you've done all the talking. You told me of your life, now I'll tell you about mine. We should know each other completely before we begin to travel together.

JEAN   Just a moment. Forgive me--but won't you regret it later if you tell me your dearest secrets?

JULIE   Aren't you my friend?

JEAN   Yes; sometimes. But don't depend on it.

JULIE   You're not serious. Besides everyone knows my secrets. You see, my mother wasn't an aristocrat, she was from a perfectly ordinary family. But she was brought up with notions of equality, women's liberation, and all that, and she hated the thought of marriage. So when my father proposed to her she told him she would never be his wife--but she married him eventually. As far as I can tell, she never wanted me. I was left to myself, except that I had to learn everything a boy normally learns, just to show that a woman can be as good as a man. I wore boy's clothes, learned to tend horses instead of dairy work. I groomed them, and I was made to go hunting. I even had to learn to plough. All the women on the estate were made to do men's work, and the men had to do the women's. As a result the property was almost bankrupt and we were the laughingstock of the countryside.

Finally my father seems to have come to his senses, and he fought back: everything was changed, and done the way he wanted. My mother fell ill--I don't know what was the matter--but she often had fits, she shut herself up in the attic or wandered out into the grounds at night. Then we had the great fire you've heard people talk about. The house, the stables, and the barn all burned down. It looked deliberate--because it happened the day after the insurance ran out, and though my father had sent in the new premium, the messenger got held up somewhere and never arrived in time.

(She fills her glass and drinks from it.)

JEAN   Haven't you had enough?

JULIE   Oh, it doesn't matter! We were destitute. We had to sleep in the coaches, and my father had no idea how he was going to pay to rebuild the house. Then my mother suggested he ask for a loan from one of her childhood friends, a brickmaker living nearby. My father got the loan, and was astonished to get it free of interest. Then the estate was rebuilt. (Drinks again.) Do you know who burned it down?

JEAN   Your mother.

JULIE   Do you know who the brickmaker was?

JEAN   Her lover.

JULIE   Do you know whose money it was?

JEAN   Let me see...no, I don't.

JULIE   It was my mother's.

JEAN   And therefore the Count's.

JULIE   No. They never made a marriage settlement. My mother had a small inheritance which she wanted to keep out of my father's hands, so she invested it--with her friend.

JEAN   Who stole it.

JULIE   Exactly. He kept it. My father eventually found out about it all, but he couldn't go to law, he couldn't repay the money, and he couldn't prove that it had been his wife's all along. He tried to shoot himself--at least, at least people said he tried, but he couldn't do it. So he survived, and my mother had to pay for her conspiracy. We had five awful years. I sympathized with my father, but I took my mother's side because I didn't understand what had happened. She taught me to distrust men and to hate them. I promised her never to be the slave of any man.

JEAN   And yet you got engaged to that attorney.

JULIE Just so that he would become my slave!

JEAN And wouldn't he?

JULIE He would have soon enough, but I wouldn't have him. He bored me.

JEAN I saw it happen--out by the stables.

JULIE What did you see?

JEAN I saw how he broke off the engagement!

JULIE That's a lie! I broke it off. If he says he did, he's a scoundrel.

JEAN No, he's not a scoundrel. You do hate men, don't you Miss Julie?

JULIE Yes, most of them. But sometimes I'm weak, and then...

JEAN Do you hate me too?

JULIE Beyond limit! I would kill you like an animal...

JEAN Shoot me as one shoots a mad dog?

JULIE Exactly!

JEAN But now you have nothing to shoot with. And no mad dog. So what shall we do?

JULIE Escape!

JEAN To torture each other?

JULIE No! I want to enjoy two days, eight days, as long as we can. And then die.

JEAN Die? That's foolish. We'd be better off setting up our hotel.

JULIE (not hearing) Lake Como, where the sun always shines, laurel trees blossom at Christmas, and the oranges gleaming...

JEAN Lake Como is a rain-sodden little hole, and I never saw an orange there outside the grocery store. But it's a good tourist trap. Plenty of villas to rent out to couples--it's a quick way to make a profit. They take out a six-month contract, and then leave after three weeks!

JULIE Why?

JEAN They fall out, of course! But the rent has to be paid just the same. And then you rent out the villa again--because love endures--

though not for very long.

JULIE   You won't die with me?

JEAN   I don't want to die at all. I enjoy life, and besides, suicide is a crime against the providence which gave us life.

JULIE   You believe in God?

JEAN   Of course I do. I go to church every other Sunday. But to tell the truth, I'm tired of all this talking. I'm going to bed.

JULIE   Do you think I'll put up with that? Don't you know a man owes something to the woman he has humiliated?

JEAN   (throws a silver coin on the table) Here! I don't want to owe anyone anything!

JULIE   (apparently not noticing) Do you know what the law says...

JEAN   Unfortunately the law has no penalty for the woman who seduces a man.

JULIE   What can we do, but escape, marry, and then separate?

JEAN   Supposing I refuse to enter this mesalliance.

JULIE   Mesalliance?

JEAN   Yes; you see, I have better ancestors than you. None of mine committed arson.

JULIE   How do you know?

JEAN   Well, you can't prove me wrong--we don't keep any family records-- except with the police. But I've seen your family tree in that book on the drawing-room table. Do you know who your first ancestor was? A miller, who let his wife sleep with the king during the Danish wars. My ancestors weren't like that. I have no ancestors--instead, I'll become an ancestor myself.

JULIE   I gave my heart to a scoundrel, gave my family honor...

JEAN   Dishonor! I told you not to drink so much. It makes you talk, and it's a bad idea to talk too much.

JULIE   I know that now--but if only you loved me...

JEAN   For the last time, what do you mean? Am I supposed to burst into tears, jump over your riding crop, kiss your foot, dally with you at Lake Como for three weeks, and then...what am I supposed to do? What do you want? I'm getting tired of this, but it's what always happens when you meddle with women. I know you're unhappy, I know you're having a bad time, but I don't understand what you want. We don't give ourselves your airs, and we don't hate the way you do either. We take love as a game, when work will let us, but we don't spend day and night at it as you do. I think you're sick, you must be sick.

JULIE   Now you talk like a human being. Be gentle with me.

JEAN   Yes, but act like a human being yourself. You spit on me, and you won't allow me to get my own back.

JULIE   Help me, help me. Tell me what I must do. Where can I go?

JEAN   For Christ's sake, I don't know!

JULIE   I know I've been angry, I know I've been out of my senses, but isn't there any way out?

JEAN   Stay here, and keep calm. No one knows anything.

JULIE   That's impossible. Those people know it, Kristin knows it.

JEAN   They know nothing, and they wouldn't believe it if they did.

JULIE   But--it could happen again.

JEAN   That's true.

JULIE   And there could be--consequences...

JEAN   Consequences? What's the matter with me that I didn't think of that? Yes, there is only one way--get out of here. At once. I'm not coming with you, that would wreck everything. You must go alone--wherever you like.

JULIE   Alone? Where? I can't do that!

JEAN   You must! And before the Count returns. You know what will happen. Now we've done it once, we'll keep doing it, getting more and more reckless, and before you know where we are someone will discover us. So go! Write to the Count, tell him everything--just don't tell him it was me. He'll never guess that, and I don't think he'll want to know.

JULIE   I'll go if you come with me.

JEAN   Are you insane! "Miss Julie elopes with Servant"--it would be in every paper, and the Count would never live through it.

JULIE   I can't go. I can't stay. Help me. I am so desperately tired. Order me to go. Set me in motion, because I don't know how to think or act any more.

JEAN What a poor creature you are! Why do you preen yourselves and stick your noses in the air as if you were lords of creation! Well, I'll order you. Go upstairs and dress. See that you have enough money for the journey. Then come back here.

JULIE Come up with me!

JEAN To your room! Now you are insane! (Weakening.) No! Go at once! (Leads her to the door.)

JULIE Talk gently to me, Jean.

JEAN A command is never gentle. Now you know.

(Left alone, JEAN draws a sigh of relief. Then he sits at the table, takes out a notebook and pencil. Now and then he reckons aloud. KRISTIN enters, dressed for church, and carrying his cape and neckerchief.)

KRISTIN Lord Jesus, what a mess this place looks! What have you been doing?

JEAN Miss Julie brought the crowd in. You mean you slept right through it?

KRISTIN I slept like a log.

JEAN You're already dressed for church!

KRISTIN You promised to come to the service with me.

JEAN So I did. Well, you've brought my cape, so let's go.

(KRISTIN begins to dress him in his cape and neckerchief.)

What's the sermon today?

KRISTIN If I remember rightly, the beheading of John the Baptist.

JEAN (sleepy) That will be so long! Ouch, you're choking me! I'm so sleepy, so sleepy.

KRISTIN What were you doing up all night? You look washed out.

JEAN I sat here talking to Miss Julie.

KRISTIN That girl doesn't know what's proper.

JEAN Kristin, listen.

KRISTIN Well?

JEAN It's strange, whichever way you look at it. Her!

KRISTIN What's so strange?

JEAN Everything.

(Pause. KRISTIN notices the half-empty glasses.)

KRISTIN Have you been drinking with her too?

JEAN Yes.

KRISTIN No! Look at me! Is it possible? Is it possible?

JEAN (after a moment) Yes--it's possible.

KRISTIN I would never have believed it. No, no, no.

JEAN You're not jealous of her, are you?

KRISTIN Jealous? No, not of her. If it had been Clara or Sofi I'd have scratched their eyes out. But this is--dirty!

JEAN Are you angry with her?

KRISTIN No, with you! It was wrong, as wrong as could be. Poor girl. Does anyone know? I won't stay in this house any longer. Not if I can't respect the family.

JEAN Why should you respect them?

KRISTIN Oh, you're so clever! Do you want to work for people who behave like that? What? It's a disgrace to work for them.

JEAN But it's worthwhile just to know they're no better than we are.

KRISTIN I don't think so. If they're no better than we are, what's the point of us trying to improve? And think of the Count! After all the trouble he's had. No, I won't stay! And with someone like you! If it had been with the attorney, with some better man...

JEAN What?

KRISTIN Oh, you're all right in your way, but there's a difference between people. I can't get over it. She was always so proud, so standoffish--you'd never expect her to give in to a man like you! She wanted to shoot Diana for going after the gamekeeper's pug! Well, I tell you, I won't stay here. October 24th, and I'm leaving.

JEAN And then what will you do?

KRISTIN Well, if you want to know, if we're getting married it's about time you found something else.

JEAN   What sort of thing? I can't get this sort of job if I'm married.

KRISTIN   I know that. Get a job with the State, as a porter or a factory caretaker. I know they don't pay much, but the job would be safe, and the wife and children get a pension...

JEAN   Well, thanks very much, but it's not exactly in my line to think of dying for a wife and children just yet. I had something rather better in mind.

KRISTIN   I know all about your plans; what about your responsibilities? Think of them.

JEAN   You don't have to tell me what my responsibilities are. I know well enough what I should do. But we can talk about this later. If you're ready, let's get to church.

KRISTIN   Who's that wandering about up there?

JEAN   I don't know, unless it's Clara.

KRISTIN (leaving)   Would the Count be home already, without us knowing?

JEAN (afraid)   The Count! No, it can't be him, he would have rung for me!

KRISTIN   Well, God help us, I've never known anything like this.

(KRISTIN goes to her room. The sun is now shining through the treetops in the grounds, and eventually reaches into the kitchen. JEAN goes to the door and gives a sign. JULIE appears in traveling clothes, carrying a small birdcage covered with a cloth. She places this on a chair.)

JULIE   I'm ready.

JEAN   Quiet! Kristin is awake!

JULIE (nervous)   Does she suspect anything?

JEAN   She **knows** nothing at all. My God, you look terrible.

JULIE   What's the matter?

JEAN   You're as white as a corpse--and you've got dirt on your face.

JULIE   I **can** wash it off. (Washes her face in the handbowl.) Give me a towel. Oh, the sun's coming up.

JEAN   Yes. Now the evil spirits disappear.

JULIE   The evil spirits have been out tonight. Jean, come with me. I can pay.

MISS JULIE

JEAN (doubtfully)   Do you have enough?

JULIE   Enough to begin with. Come with me. I can't travel alone today of all days. Midsummer's Day! On a stifling train, packed in with crowds of people, all staring at me. Hanging around at stations when you're desperate to move on. I can't do it! With all my memories coming back: midsummer days in my childhood, with the church covered with birch and lilac, the dinner table laid, relatives, friends, dancing in the grounds, music, flowers, and games. No matter where we go, I shall take those memories with me, and the awful, bitter, pangs of conscience!

JEAN   I'll come--but now, at once, before it's too late. This minute.

JULIE   Then get ready! (Picks up the birdcage.)

JEAN   No, no baggage! We don't want anything in our way.

JULIE   I'm only taking enough for the compartment.

JEAN   What's that? What is it?

JULIE   Only my greenfinch. I don't want to leave it.

JEAN   What? Are you mad! We're not taking a bird with us. Put it down!

JULIE   It's the only thing I own in this house, the only living thing I have since Diana was unfaithful to me. Don't be cruel; let me take it!

JEAN   Put it down I say! And don't shout. Kristin will hear us.

JULIE   I won't leave it in the hands of strangers! I'd rather kill it!

JEAN   Then get it out! I'll smash its head off!

JULIE   Don't hurt it! Oh, I can't, I can't!

JEAN   I can! Bring it here!

(JULIE takes the bird from its cage.)

JULIE   My darling little Serine! Must you leave your mistress now?

JEAN   For God's sake, no scenes! It's for your own good. Now, quickly! (Snatches the bird from her, takes it to the chopping block.) You should have learned to butcher chickens instead of firing a revolver! Then you wouldn't faint at the sight of blood.

(He chops the bird's head off.)

JULIE (screams)   Kill me, too! Kill me, too! If you can butcher an innocent creature without a tremor. I hate you, detest you! There is blood between us. I wish I had never set eyes on you. I wish I had never been born!

JEAN   What's the use of wishing! We have to go!

JULIE (approaching the block as if drawn against her will)   No, I will not go! I can't... I must look... Listen, there's a carriage out there!... Do you think I can't stand the sight of blood, do you think I'm so helpless... Oh, I'd give anything to see your blood, your brains smashed on a wooden block. I'd like to see your whole sex swimming like that in its blood. By God, I'd like to wade knee-deep through your guts, and drink your blood from your skull, I'd like to see your heart burned and roasted like mutton! You think I'm helpless; you think I love you, because my womb called for your seed-- you think I'll carry your children under my heart, feed them with my blood, and give them your name! Well, what is your name? I never heard it. Do you have one? What would I be--Madame Gatekeeper? Mistress Dunghill? You dog in my collar, you peasant in my livery! And I share you with my cook, compete with scullions for your favor! Oh!--do you think I'll run like a coward? I'll stay here until the roof falls in! My father will get home, find his desk ransacked, his money gone--and he'll ring the bell--that bell!--twice--for his manservant! And then he'll send for the law, and I shall tell him everything. God, it will be a relief to be finished with it all, all! If only it is finished. He'll have a stroke, he'll die, and we'll all be finished, every one of us, and I can have some peace...calm...eternal rest. The coat-of-arms will be smashed across the coffin, the Count's line at an end. But the servant goes on! Spawned in the orphanage, he wins laurels in the gutter, and distinction in the jail!

JEAN   Well done, Miss Julie! There speaks the royal blood! But for God's sake don't spill the beans now!

(KRISTIN enters, carrying a hymnbook. JULIE rushes to her and falls as if seeking shelter in her arms.)

JULIE   Help me, Kristin, help me against this man!

KRISTIN (coldly)   What kind of behavior is this for a Sunday morning? (Sees the blood.) Have you been slaughtering pigs in here? Why all the screaming and hysterics?

JULIE   You're my friend. You're a woman. Don't let that scoundrel fool you!

JEAN (softly)   While you ladies talk, I think I'll have a shave.

(He goes quietly off to the right.)

JULIE   You must understand me! Listen to me!

KRISTIN   I don't understand this kind of thing at all. Why are you

MISS JULIE

dressed for traveling? And he was standing there with his hat on! What are you both up to?

JULIE   Listen to me, Kristin, listen to me, I'll tell you everything!

KRISTIN   I don't want to know!

JULIE   You must listen! I want to talk to you...

KRISTIN   What about? If it's about your fooleries with Jean, I don't care and I don't want to know. But if you're trying to trap him into bolting, I'll put a stop to that.

JULIE   Calm down, and listen to me, Kristin! I can't stay here. Jean can't stay here. We must all go--all three of us--to Switzerland. We can set up a hotel together. I have the money--Jean and I would run it, and you--I thought you would take on the kitchen. Wouldn't that be fine? Say yes, now, and come with us! Everything is settled! So come!

(Throws her arms around KRISTIN, who remains cold and thoughtful.)

(Presto tempo.) You've never been anywhere, Kristin--you ought to see the world. You can't believe what fun it is to go by train--new people all the time--new countries--and when we get to Hamburg we can go to the zoo, you'd like that--and the theaters and opera--and in Munich we can go to the museums, with Rubens and Raphael, you know, the great painters. You've heard of Munich--where King Ludwig lived--the king who went mad--we could see his castle--it's still there, just the same as it is in the fairy tales--And then it's not far to Switzerland--over the Alps, with snow even at midsummer--and oranges and laurel trees, green all the year round.

(JEAN can be seen, right, sharpening his razor on a strop, which he holds in his teeth and his left hand as he listens contentedly to the conversation and nods approval from time to time.)

(Prestissimo.) And then we take a hotel--and I'll sit at the desk while Jean welcomes the guests. We can go shopping, write letters--oh, what a life!--trains whistling and buses coming and going, bells ringing in the rooms and in the restaurant--and I can write out the bills--oh, I can fix those!--you would never believe what cowards people are when they have to pay their bill!--and you--you'd be chief cook--you wouldn't have to do anything, of course--you'd be dressed in the latest fashion, and when people saw you--with your good looks--I'm not flattering you--one fine day you would catch yourself a husband, a rich Englishman--people are so easy to (Slowing.)--trap--and then we would be rich and build ourselves a villa on Lake Como--of course it rains a little sometimes--but (Falling off.)--the sun will shine sometimes--even though it seems dark outside--and--then--if we want to we could come home again--come back-- (Pause.)--here--or some other place...

KRISTIN   Do you believe all that yourself?

JULIE (exhausted)   Do I believe it myself? I don't know. I don't believe anything any more. Nothing. Nothing at all!

(She falls onto the bench and lays her head in her arms on the table. JEAN returns. He lays his razor on the table.)

KRISTIN   So you were going to run for it!

JEAN   Run for it? You've already heard. You heard what Miss Julie said. Even though she's worn out after a long night, there's something to be said for her plans.

KRISTIN   Listen to you! Do you think I'd cook for that...

JEAN (sharply)   When you talk of your mistress you'll guard your tongue! Understand?

KRISTIN   My mistress!

JEAN   Yes!

KRISTIN   Do you know what you're saying?

JEAN   Yes: and you'd do better to listen and hold your tongue. Miss Julie is your mistress: if you despise her you despise yourself.

KRISTIN   I've always had enough self-respect...

JEAN   To despise others!

KRISTIN   I've never sunk below my place. Tell me when the Count's cook had anything to do with the groom or the swineherd. Tell me that!

JEAN   You had the good luck to find a decent man.

KRISTIN   Oh yes! Was it a decent man who stole the Count's oats from the stable!

JEAN   Can you talk? Didn't you steal spices to bribe your family with?

KRISTIN   What did you say?

JEAN   And you can't look up to your employers any more! You!

KRISTIN   Are you coming to church or aren't you? You could use a good sermon after tonight!

JEAN   No, I'm not going to church today. Go by yourself, and confess your own faults.

MISS JULIE

KRISTIN   I'll do that! And I'll come home forgiven. There is forgiveness for you too; the Savior suffered and died on the cross for our sins, and if we approach Him in faith and a repentant spirit He takes all our guilt upon him.

JEAN   Including the spices...?

JULIE   Do you believe that, Kristin?

KRISTIN   As truly as I stand here. It's my living faith, the faith of my childhood and my youth. And where sin abounds, grace abounds also...

JULIE   Oh if only I had your faith!

KRISTIN   But you can't have it, Miss Julie, without God's special grace, and not everyone is given it.

JULIE   Who does have it then?

KRISTIN   That's the great secret of grace. God is no respecter of persons. The last shall be first...

JULIE   Then he respects those who are most wretched...

KRISTIN   ...and it is easier for a camel to go through the eye of a needle than for a rich man to enter into the kingdom of God. You see, Miss Julie, that's how it is. Anyway, I'm going on my own--and I'll tell the groom not to release any of the horses, just in case anyone should want to go before the Count comes home! Good-bye! (Exits.)

JEAN   The bitch! And all this for the sake of a greenfinch!

JULIE (dully)   Let the greenfinch be! Can you see any way out of this, any end?

JEAN   No.

JULIE   What would you do in my place?

JEAN   In your place? Let me see. A lady, who has--fallen. I'm not sure. Yes, I know!

JULIE (takes the razor, gestures)   Like this?

JEAN   Yes! But not for me! Because, you know, there is a difference between us.

JULIE   Because you're a man and I'm a woman? Is that what you mean? What sort of difference is that?

JEAN   Well, it's the same difference as--well, between a man and a woman!

JULIE. I want to do it, but I can't! Nor could my father, when he should have.

JEAN No, he should not have done it! He had to have his revenge first.

JULIE And now my mother has hers--through me.

JEAN Did you ever love your father, Miss Julie?

JULIE Oh yes, endlessly! But I hated him too. I must have hated him, even without knowing it. But it was my father who gave me my contempt for my own sex, he made me half woman and half man. Whose fault is all this? My father's, my mother's, or my own? My own? Blame myself, when I have no self left? I don't have an idea except from my father, I don't have a passion except those given to me by my mother, and as for people being equal--I got that from him, my fiancé-- which is why he was a scoundrel! How can it be my fault? Shoulder the guilt onto Jesus, as Kristin does? I can't! I'm too proud, too intelligent--thanks to my father's teaching--and it's a lie that the rich man cannot enter the kingdom of God, because Kristin has money in the savings bank, so how does she get in? Whose fault? What does it matter to us whose fault it is? I am the one who has to bear the guilt and the consequences.

JEAN Yes, but...

(Two sharp rings from the bell. JULIE starts to her feet. JEAN begins to change his coat.)

The Count! He's home! Do you think Kristin...

(Goes to the speaking tube to listen. The audience does not hear the Count, but JEAN replies from time to time.)

JULIE Has he been to his desk yet?

JEAN Jean, your excellency!... Yes, your excellency!... Yes, in half an hour!

JULIE What's he saying, what's he saying!

JEAN He wants his coffee and his boots in half an hour.

JULIE Half an hour! But I'm so tired. I can't do anything: can't feel guilt, can't escape, can't stay, live, or die! Give me your orders, and I'll obey them like a dog. Give me my last commands, save my honor, save his name! You know what I should do, but I can't! Will you, will you, order me to do it!

JEAN I don't know! I can't do anything either--nothing makes sense. It's as if this coat made me... I can't order you to do anything!

MISS JULIE   45

Since the Count talked to me... Oh, this damned peasant crouched on my back!--I believe if the Count came down here now and ordered me to cut my throat I'd do it on the spot!

JULIE Then pretend that you are the Count and I am you. You could act well enough to fall on your knees before me--you played the nobleman then--or... Have you ever seen a hypnotist at the theater? He says to his subject, "Pick up that broom," and he does so. He says, "Sweep!" and he sweeps.

JEAN But the subject must be asleep!

JULIE I am asleep! The whole room is in smoke. You look like an iron stove--like a darkclad man in a top hat--and your eyes shine like coals after the flames have gone--and your face a white blur like fallen ashes-- (The sun has now fallen on Jean.)--so warm, so cosy--so light, so peaceful...

(She rubs her hands as if they were stretched before a fire. JEAN places the razor in her hand, and whispers into her ear.)

JEAN Here is the broom. Now, go out into the light, out into the barn...

JULIE (awake) Thank you! I am going to rest. But tell me that the first can be given the gift of grace. Tell me you believe that.

JEAN The first? No, I can't say that. But Miss Julie... You are no longer one of the first. You are among the lowest...

JULIE That's true! I am among the lowest of all. But now... I can't go. Tell me again that I must.

JEAN No, I can't do that either. I can't.

JULIE And the first shall be last...

JEAN Don't think! Don't think! You're taking away all my strength and making me a coward!--Oh, I thought the bell moved! No! Let me stick some paper in it. To be so afraid of a bell! But it's not the bell--there's something behind it--a hand that sets the bells in motion--and there's something behind the hand that sets it in motion! Block your ears, block your ears! But then it's worse still, it keeps ringing, ringing, until it's answered! And then it's too late. He'll send for the law, and then...

(Two sharp rings on the bell. JEAN pulls himself together at once.)

It's ghastly! But there is no other way! Go!

(MISS JULIE walks firmly out through the doorway.)

THE STRONGER

THE STRONGER

(MRS. X enters, wearing a winter hat and cape, and carrying a wicker basket on her arm. She sees two tables, at one of which sits MISS Y, before a half-empty bottle of beer, reading an illustrated magazine. From time to time she picks up another.)

<u>MRS. X</u>   Amelia, darling! <u>Alone</u> on Christmas Eve, like a poor bachelor!

(MISS Y looks up from her magazine, nods, and continues to read.)

It hurts me to look at you, all alone, alone in a café on Christmas Eve! It's as bad as a wedding party I saw come into a restaurant once. The bride sat down to read some scandal sheet, and the groom played billiards with the witnesses! What a **beginning**, I thought! How will it all end! Playing billiards on his wedding day! And she sat reading that trash! That wouldn't do for me!

(A WAITRESS enters with a cup of hot chocolate, which she places in front of MRS X.)

Do you know something, Amelia? I think, now, that you would have done better to keep him! You know I was the first to say you ought to forgive him. You do remember, don't you? You could have been married by now, with a home of your own. Oh, last Christmas, do you remember how happy you were, out there in the country with his parents? How you longed to get away from the theater to the happiness of a home. Yes, darling, the home is always best--next to the theater, that is...and children...but you wouldn't understand that.

(MISS Y contemptuous. MRS. X takes a few sips from her cup and opens her basket to show her Christmas gifts.)

Look what I've bought for my little ones! (Takes out a doll.) Look at this! For Lisa! Watch its eyes move, and its head! Look at that!-- and this pop-gun is for Maja.

(She primes the pop-gun and aims it at MISS Y, who shudders.)

Are you afraid? Did you think I would shoot you? What? Bless me if I didn't think so! If <u>you</u> wanted to shoot <u>me</u> I wouldn't be surprised, after all, I did get in your way--I <u>know</u> you can never forgive me--although I was completely innocent. You still think I plotted to get you away from the Grand Theater, but I didn't, I didn't do that, although you think I did--but there, it's all the same: if I say I didn't you'll still believe I did. (Takes out a pair of embroidered slippers.) These are for my old man--I embroidered the tulips myself--I loathe tulips, of course, but he must have tulips on everything.

(Curious, MISS Y looks up sarcastically. MRS. X puts a hand in each slipper.)

Look what small feet Bob has. And such an elegant walk. Of course you've never seen him in slippers.

(She lets the slipper fall back on the table; MISS Y gives a high-pitched laugh.)

And when he's angry he stamps his foot on the floor like this. "Why can't those damned servants ever learn to make a cup of coffee. The cretins; they haven't even trimmed the lamps properly." Or there's a draught, and his feet are freezing. "Dammit, it's cold, and the idiots can't keep the fire going properly."

(She rubs the sole of one slipper against the upper side of the other. MISS Y laughs loudly.)

Then he comes home and looks for his slippers, and Mary has put them under the dresser...oh, but it's shameful to sit here and mock one's husband like this. And he is kind, a good little husband... Amelia, you should have such a husband. Why are you laughing at me? Why? Anyway, I know he's faithful to me, I know that. He told me so himself. What are you sniggering at? When I was on tour in Norway, that hussy Frederica tried to seduce him—can you imagine it? (Pause.) I would have scratched her eyes out if she'd come near the place while I was home. (Pause.) But I'm glad Bob told me himself, so that I didn't pick it up as gossip. (Pause.) Frederica isn't the only one, believe me. I don't know why, but women are always foolish about _my_ husband! They must think he can engage them, just because he's on the management. Perhaps you've had a go at him yourself!— I never more that half-believed you—but now I know he never bothered himself with you. And I know you bear a grudge against him.

(Pause. They watch each other awkwardly.)

Come and see us this evening, Amelia; show us that you're not angry with us, or at least with me. I can't tell you how awful it is not to be friends, with _you_ especially. Perhaps it's because I once got in your way (Slowing down.) or—I don't know why... I don't know at all.

(Pause. MISS Y stares curiously at MRS. X.)

Our friendship was so strange—when I saw you for the first time I was afraid of you, so afraid that I didn't dare let you out of my sight; no matter where I went I always found myself near you. I made you my friend because I was afraid to have you as an enemy. I was uneasy when you came to see us, because I could see my husband couldn't stand you. I felt awkward, as if I were wearing an ill-fitting dress. And I did do everything I could to persuade him to like you; it didn't work—until your engagement. Then it was as if you dared to show your true feelings for the first time, you felt secure enough to offer him affection. Then what happened? Strange, I wasn't jealous! I remember the christening; you as a god-parent, and I made him kiss you—you were so confused. Of course, I took no notice, I didn't even think twice about it. I've never thought about it since--until now! (Rising hastily.) Why don't you say something? You've said nothing all this time, you just sit there and let me talk! Watching me, unwinding my thoughts like raw silk from a cocoon. Thoughts--suspicions perhaps--let me think. Why did you break off your engagement? Why haven't you been to the house since then? Why won't you come this evening?

(MISS Y looks as if she is about to speak.)

Never mind! You needn't say anything, I understand it all myself! Because, because, because now we're even! Oh, I won't sit at the same table with you! (Moves her things to the other table.) That was why I had to cover everything with tulips. I hate tulips--but you like them! (Throws the slippers onto the floor.) We had to spend our summers at the lake--because you don't like the sea! We christened our son Eskil--because Eskil is your father's name! I had to wear your favorite colors, read your favorite authors, eat your favorite dishes, drink your favorite drinks--even your chocolate, for example! Oh my God, it's grotesque even to think of it, grotesque! Everything we have was yours, even your passions! Your very soul crept into mine like a maggot into an apple, eating and eating, digging, digging, until all you left was a husk and a little mold. I wanted to escape from you, but I couldn't; you lay like a snake, enchanting me with your dark eyes. I tried to lift my wings, and I could feel you pulling me down. As I lay in the water, you bound my feet, and the more I thrashed my arms about to try to swim, the deeper down I worked myself, till I sank to the mud where you waited for me like some huge crab ready to seize me with its claws. And I'm lying there now!

    I hate you, hate you, hate you! And you, you just sit there, silent, calm, indifferent; indifferent to past or present, Christmas or New Year, indifferent to others' happiness or unhappiness. You don't know how to hate, you don't know how to love; still as a stork in front of a rat-hole. You didn't know how to seize your prey for yourself, you couldn't do that, so you simply waited it out. And here you sit in your own special corner--did you know people called it the rat-trap because of you--reading your magazines in the hope of finding someone in distress, some poor wretch newly dismissed from the theater. You sit here like some crazy pilot counting shipwrecks, receiving every personal disaster as an offering to you!

    Poor Amelia! It hurts me as much as it hurts you. I know you're unhappy, unhappy because you've been hurt, and evil because you've been hurt. I'd like to be angry with you; but I can't--even though you're still a little--yes, that little matter with Bob, it doesn't even worry me--what has it to do with me! What does it matter whether you or anyone else taught me to drink chocolate. (Drinks from her cup with distaste.) Besides, chocolate is good for you. And if I learned to dress like you--well, so much the better--it just binds my husband more strongly to me--which makes you the loser, me the winner; in fact, if I read things rightly, you've already lost him. You wanted me out of the way, and you got me out of the way, and now you sit here and regret it. I don't regret it; after all, we shouldn't be petty about it, should we? At least I don't have to take something that no one else wants!

Perhaps, at this moment, when all's said and done, I am the stronger. You never took a thing from me, you were only giving away everything *you* had--and now I'm like a thief in the night; when you awoke I owned everything that you once had.

Why did everything always turn worthless and sterile in your hands? With your tulips and your passions, you couldn't keep a man's love. I could. All your favorite authors couldn't make you learn life's lessons. I did. You never had a son named Eskil, even though your father's name was Eskil.

And why are you always silent, silent? Yes, I thought it was a sign of strength; but perhaps you simply couldn't think of anything to say. (Rising, picking up the slippers.) Now I'm going home-- taking the tulips with me--your tulips! You could never learn a thing from others, you could never bend--and you broke like a dry reed-- but I **didn't!**

Thank you, Amelia, for everything you've taught me; and thank you for teaching my husband how to love. Now I shall go home--to love him.

A DREAM PLAY

MEMORANDUM

In this dream play, as in the earlier dream play To Damascus, the author has sought to imitate the disconnected yet apparently logical structure of a dream. Anything may happen, everything is possible and probable. Time and space do not exist; on the basis of an insignificant reality the imagination develops to weave new patterns, a blend of memory, experience, free association, the absurd, and improvisation. The characters split, double, multiply, vanish, blur, merge, assimilate one another. But a single consciousness rules over them all, that of the dreamer; for there are no secrets, no incongruities, no scruples, and no law. He judges no one, defends no one, simply narrates; and since the dream is generally painful, and only rarely pleasant, a tone of melancholy and compassion for all living creatures rules the swaying narrative. Sleep, the liberator, is often painful, but when the torture is at its worst, awakening comes and reconciles the sufferer with reality, which, however painful it may be, at that moment seems a pleasure compared with the torments of dream.

August Strindberg

(An overhanging cloud bank resembling precipitous mountaintops, ruined castles and fortresses. The constellations of Leo, Virgo, and Libra are visible, the planet Jupiter shining brightly among them.

On the summit of the highest cloud stands INDRA'S DAUGHTER.)

INDRA'S VOICE (from above)   Daughter, where are you?

DAUGHTER   Here, Father, here!

INDRA'S VOICE   My child, you have gone astray, you are sinking. Take care. How did you come here?

DAUGHTER   Borne on a cloud, I followed the lightning flash,
Sinking downwards from high eternity.
Tell me, Father, to what realms have I come?
Why is this air so close, so hard to breathe?

INDRA'S VOICE
Far from the morning star and the second world,
You have entered the third, the atmosphere of earth;
There, in the seventh house, Libra gives the sign
That the daystar stands at autumn's balance,
Where day and night are equal.

DAUGHTER   Is this the earth? This dark and heavy world
Lit only by the moon?

INDRA'S VOICE
Of all the spheres that wander space,
This is the heaviest and most dense.

DAUGHTER   And does it never see the sun?

INDRA'S VOICE
The sun shines there, but not forever.

DAUGHTER   The clouds are parting, and I see...

INDRA'S VOICE
What do you see, my child?

DAUGHTER   I see that it is fair... I see green forests,
Blue waters, mountains, golden fields...

INDRA'S VOICE
Yes, it is fair, like all that Brahma shaped.
Once, in the dawn of time, it was more fair.
Then something happened, perhaps a change of course,
Rebellion, crime, and punishment...

DAUGHTER   I hear them. What kind of race...?

INDRA'S VOICE	Go there, and see. I cannot blame the children of the gods, And yet the tongue you hear is theirs.
DAUGHTER	It sounds... There is no pleasure in those cries!
INDRA'S VOICE	No. That tongue you hear, their mother tongue, Is called Complaint. A discontented, thankless race.
DAUGHTER	Do not say so! For I can hear Cries of joy, thunder and lightning, Ringing bells; I see them lighting fires, And voices in their thousands Singing praise and thanks to heaven. (Pause.) You judge them too severely, Father.
INDRA'S VOICE	Go there, and see, and hear, and then return. Tell me if their complaints have reason, And justify their endless groaning.
DAUGHTER	Well, I will go; but come with me, Father!
INDRA'S VOICE	I cannot breathe their air.
DAUGHTER	Now the cloud sinks, the air grows dense. I am choking! This is not air, but smoke and water, Dragging me downwards by their weight, downwards! The world is spinning! This world is not the best!
INDRA'S VOICE	Not the best, indeed, but not the worst. Its name is Dust; and, spinning like the others, It grips its race in dizzy madness, and bewilderment. Have courage, Daughter, you shall prove yourself.
DAUGHTER	I am sinking!

*

(A forest of giant hollyhocks in bloom: white, crimson, yellow, and violet. Over their heads can be seen the gilded roof of a castle with a flower bud crowning its summit. At the foot of the castle walls are dung-heaps and straw, the litter from the castle stables. On each side of the stage, remaining there for the whole play, are stylized flats, representing simultaneously a room, architecture, and landscape.

Enter DAUGHTER and GLAZIER.)

DAUGHTER   The castle is still growing. Can you see how much it's grown since last year?

GLAZIER (to himself) I have never seen that castle in my life before, and I've never heard of a castle growing...but... (To DAUGHTER, with conviction.) Yes, it's grown a good six feet! They've obviously manured it. Look! There's a new wing growing on the sunny side!

DAUGHTER It ought to flower soon, it's already past midsummer.

GLAZIER Can't you see that bud up there?

DAUGHTER (clapping her hands) Yes, yes, I see it! Tell me, why do flowers blossom from the dirt?

GLAZIER (solemnly) They cannot bear dirt! And so they grow as fast as they can towards the light. To blossom--and to die.

DAUGHTER Who lives in the castle?

GLAZIER I did know...but I've forgotten...

DAUGHTER I believe there is a prisoner there! Sitting there, waiting... waiting for me to rescue him! And I shall!

GLAZIER But think of the cost.

DAUGHTER Do you ask the cost of what you _have_ to do? Let's go to the castle!

GLAZIER Very well.

*

(As they go upstage, the back wall slowly opens. The scene is a simple bare room with a table and a few chairs. At the table sits the OFFICER in a highly unconventional modern uniform. He rocks to and fro on his chair, hacking the table with his sword.)

DAUGHTER (slowly taking the sword from him) Don't do that! Don't do that!

OFFICER Dear Agnes, let me keep the sword!

DAUGHTER No, you're ruining the table! (To GLAZIER.) Go down to the harness-room and put in that new window. I'll see you later.

(Exit GLAZIER.)

You are a prisoner in your own room. I have come to set you free!

OFFICER I thought you would come, but...I wasn't sure you would want to.

A DREAM PLAY

DAUGHTER Because the castle is strong, with seven walls? But it had to be done. Now, will you come or not?

OFFICER To tell the truth, I don't know! Whatever happens I'm bound to suffer. Every joy in life has to be paid for with a double measure of sorrow. It's hard for me to stay here, but if I bought joy and freedom now, I should only have to suffer and suffer and suffer to make up for it. Agnes, I can bear it...if only I can see you!

DAUGHTER What do you see in me?

OFFICER Beauty, the harmony of the universe! In your form I see lines which I have seen only in the movement of the stars, in the melody of strings, in the vibration of the light! You are a child of heaven.

DAUGHTER And so are you.

OFFICER Then why should I groom horses? Clean the stables, and tend the dung-heaps?

DAUGHTER So that you will long to be free!

OFFICER I long to be free, but it is so hard to escape from it all...

DAUGHTER But it's your duty to seek freedom in the light!

OFFICER Duty? Life has never acknowledged a duty towards me!

DAUGHTER Do you believe that life has been unjust to you?

OFFICER Yes! It has been unjust...

*

(Voices are heard behind the screen, which is immediately drawn aside. The OFFICER and DAUGHTER watch, posed, their expressions frozen. At the table sits the MOTHER, very frail. In front of her is a lighted candle which she trims now and then. On the table lies a pile of newly mended children's underclothes which she marks with a quill pen. To the left a brown wardrobe. The FATHER enters carrying a shawl, which he offers to her. She rejects it.)

FATHER Don't you want it?

MOTHER What use is a shawl to me, dear friend, when I am dying?

FATHER Do you believe what the doctor said?

MOTHER I believe what he said, but I believe still more in the voice that speaks within me.

FATHER   Then it is serious. And first and last, you think of your children!

MOTHER   They have been my life and my justification...my joy and my sorrow.

FATHER   Kristina, forgive me...for everything!

MOTHER   For what? Forgive me, my dear. We have always tormented one another. Why? Who knows! There was nothing else we could do!... Well, here are the children's clothes. They must change them twice a week, Wednesdays and Saturdays, and you must see that Louisa washes the children, all over. Are you going out?

FATHER   I have to be at the college at eleven.

MOTHER   Ask Alfred to come in before you go.

FATHER (pointing to the OFFICER)   But my dear, Alfred is already here.

MOTHER   Oh, I am beginning to see badly too! Yes, it's getting darker... (Trimming the candle.) Alfred, come here!

*

(The FATHER goes out, waving good-bye.)

*

MOTHER   Who is that girl?

OFFICER (whispering)   That's Agnes!

MOTHER   Agnes? Do you know what people are saying? That she is Indra's daughter, that she begged to be allowed to come down to earth to feel as human beings feel. But don't say anything about it!

OFFICER   She is a child of god.

MOTHER (aloud)   Alfred, I shall soon leave you and your brothers and sisters. Let me give you one piece of advice.

OFFICER (sadly)   Yes, mother, what is it?

MOTHER   Only a word: don't quarrel with God!

OFFICER   What do you mean, mother?

A DREAM PLAY

MOTHER   You are not to feel that life has treated you harshly.

OFFICER   But life has treated me harshly...

MOTHER   Oh I know! You're thinking of the time when you were unfairly punished; we accused you of taking money, and afterwards we found it.

OFFICER   Yes! That injustice has damaged me for life...

MOTHER   Very well. Now go to that cupboard...

OFFICER   (ashamed)   You know about that!

MOTHER   The Swiss Family Robinson! Which--

OFFICER   Don't say any more!

MOTHER   Which you tore to pieces and hid! And for which your brother was blamed and punished!

OFFICER   To think that that cupboard can still be there after twenty years! We have moved so many times. And my mother died ten years ago!

MOTHER   And what difference does that make! You question everything, you take nothing as it is, and so you ruin all the best things in life. There's Lina!

*

LINA   Oh Madam, I am grateful, but I just can't go to the christening!

MOTHER   Why not, child?

LINA   I have nothing to wear.

MOTHER   You can borrow my shawl.

LINA   Oh, I couldn't do that...

MOTHER   I don't understand. It's not likely I'll be going anywhere!

*

OFFICER   What will father say? That was a present from him.

MOTHER   Oh what small minds!

*

FATHER (looking in)   Are you going to lend my present to a serving-girl?

MOTHER   Don't talk like that! I was a serving-girl myself at one time, and you know it. Why should you hurt innocent people?

FATHER   Why should you hurt me, your husband?

MOTHER   Oh life! Whatever good you try to do, there's always someone to get hurt. You help one person, injure another. Life!

(She trims the candle, and accidentally puts it out. The stage darkens and the screen is replaced.)

*

DAUGHTER   Oh, it's so pitiful to be human!

OFFICER   You think so?

DAUGHTER   Yes, life is hard; but love conquers everything! Come and see.

*

(At the back of the stage we see a derelict wall. In the wall is a gateway from which an alleyway leads to a green, airy square in which grows a colossal blue monkshood. To the left of the gate sits the GATEKEEPER with a shawl over her head and shoulders, knitting a star-patterned coverlet. On the right is a billboard which is being cleaned by the BILLSTICKER. Beside him is a fishing net with a green handle. Further to the right is a door containing a window shaped like a four-leafed clover. To the left of the gate stands a small lime tree with a pitch-black trunk and a few small leaves; nearby, the entrance to a cellar.

DAUGHTER (going to GATEKEEPER)   Isn't that coverlet ready yet?

GATEKEEPER   No, my friend! Twenty-six years is no time at all for such a work!

DAUGHTER   And your fiancé never came back?

GATEKEEPER   No; but it wasn't his fault. Poor thing, he _had_ to go. Thirty years ago!

DAUGHTER (to BILLSTICKER)   Was she really in the ballet? Up there at the Opera house?

A DREAM PLAY

BILLSTICKER   She was the prima ballerina...but when he went away he seemed to take her dancing with him, and so she never got another part.

DAUGHTER   Complaint! Everyone complains, some with their eyes, some with their voices...

BILLSTICKER   I don't exactly complain...at least, not now, now that I have a fishing net and a green fish box.

DAUGHTER   That makes you happy?

BILLSTICKER   Yes, so happy! It was my childhood dream! And now that it's come true... You see, I'm fifty years old...

DAUGHTER   Fifty years for a net and a fish box!

BILLSTICKER   A green one, a green one!

*

DAUGHTER (to GATEKEEPER)   Give me the shawl now. Let me sit and watch these human children! But you must stand behind me and tell me who they are.

GATEKEEPER   This is the last day of the season, and the Opera is closing down for the summer. Today they will know if they have a job next year.

DAUGHTER   Supposing they don't?

GATEKEEPER   Oh Jesus, that's a terrible sight. I always pull my shawl over my head...

DAUGHTER   Poor creatures!

GATEKEEPER   Look, here comes one of them now! She's out! You see, she's crying.

*

(The SINGER rushes through the gate holding a handkerchief to her eyes. For a moment she stops and rests her head against the wall, weeping. Then she rushes out.)

DAUGHTER   It's so pitiful to be human!

*

GATEKEEPER   But look at him! He looks happy!

*

(The OFFICER walks through the gate. He wears a frock-coat and top hat, and carries a bouquet of roses. He looks radiantly happy.)

GATEKEEPER   He's going to marry Miss Victoria...

OFFICER (downstage; looks up, sings)   Victoria!

GATEKEEPER   She'll be here at any moment.

OFFICER   Good! The carriage is waiting, the table is set, and the champagne is on ice... Ladies, let me embrace you! (He embraces DAUGHTER and GATEKEEPER. Sings.) Victoria!

WOMAN'S VOICE (above, singing)   I am here!

OFFICER (beginning to pace up and down)   Well, I will wait.

*

DAUGHTER   Do you know me?

OFFICER   No! I know only one woman, Victoria! For seven years I have come here to wait for her; at noon, when the sun beats down on the chimneys, in the evenings when darkness begins to fall. Look here on this asphalt, you can see the footsteps of a faithful lover! Hurrah! She is mine! (Sings.) Victoria! (No answer.) Now she's dressing. (To BILLSTICKER.) I see you have your fishing net; everyone at the Opera is crazy about fishing nets...or rather, about fish. Dumb fish, because they can't sing. What does a thing like that cost?

BILLSTICKER   It's rather expensive.

OFFICER (sings)   Victoria! (Shakes the lime tree.) Look, it's blossoming again--for the eighth time! (Sings.) Victoria! Now she's setting her hair. (To DAUGHTER.) Please, let me go and fetch my bride...

GATEKEEPER   No one is allowed on the stage!

OFFICER   I've been waiting here for seven years. Seven times three hundred and sixty-five makes two thousand five hundred and fifty-five! (He stops and gazes at the cloverleaf door.) I have seen that door two thousand five hundred and fifty-five times, without ever discovering where it goes! And that cloverleaf lets in the light for someone--

A DREAM PLAY

but who? Is there anyone in there? Does anyone live there?

GATEKEEPER Don't ask me. I've never seen that door opened...

OFFICER It reminds me of a pantry door I saw when I was four years old. One Sunday I went with our maidservant to another family, other maids, but I didn't get further than the kitchen, and they sat me between the water-butt and the salt-barrel. I have seen so many kitchens in my day, all of them with pantries in the corridor, and every one of them had a cloverleaf window in the door... But this can't be a pantry, because an Opera house wouldn't have a kitchen! (Sings.) Victoria! Could she have left some other way?

GATEKEEPER No, there isn't any other way out.

OFFICER Then I'm bound to meet her!

(The theater company rush by, watched by the OFFICER.)

*

OFFICER Now she'll soon be here! Look at that blue monkshood out there! I saw that when I was a child. Is it the same one? I remember going to a vicarage when I was seven years old...there were two doves, blue ones, under that monkshood...and then a bee flew into the flower and I thought to myself: now I've got you!, and I plucked the flower; but the bee stung me through the petals, and made me cry Then the vicar's wife came out and put damp earth on the sting, and we went off to get strawberries and cream for supper...I do believe it's getting dark. Where are you going?

BILLSTICKER I'm going home for supper.

OFFICER (rubbing his eyes) Supper? At this time of day? (To GATEKEEPER.) May I use your telephone for a moment? I want to put in a call to the growing castle...

DAUGHTER What do you want them for?

OFFICER I have to tell the Glazier to put in double windows; winter's coming, and I get so cold! (He goes into the Lodge.)

*

DAUGHTER Who is Victoria?

GATEKEEPER She is his sweetheart.

DAUGHTER Yes, <u>his</u> sweetheart. What she is to us or to anyone else means nothing to him.

(It grows rapidly darker.)

GATEKEEPER (lighting her lantern) It's getting dark early today!

DAUGHTER To the gods a year is but a minute!

GATEKEEPER And for men a minute can be as long as a year!

*

OFFICER (he looks shabbier, and the roses have withered) Hasn't she come yet?

GATEKEEPER No.

OFFICER But she will come, she will! (Pacing up and down.) But still, I'd better cancel dinner now...since it's evening already. Well, that's what I'd better do. (He goes in to telephone.)

*

GATEKEEPER May I have my shawl now?

DAUGHTER No, my friend, take a rest; I will do your job... I want to know men's life, I want to see if it is as hard as they say.

GATEKEEPER You realize you can't get any sleep on this job, night or day, you can never sleep...

DAUGHTER Not even at night?

GATEKEEPER Well, as much as you can manage, with that bell-rope on your arm; there are night-watchmen for the theater, and they're changed every three hours...

DAUGHTER But that's torture...

GATEKEEPER That may be so, but others would be glad to get such a job; if you knew how envied I am...

DAUGHTER Envied? People envy you this torture?

GATEKEEPER Yes! But I'll tell you what's harder than the drudgery of night-watching or the cold or the damp: all those people up there confide in me, they all come to me. Perhaps they can read the lines drawn in my face by suffering, and know I will understand. In that shawl, my friend, are hidden thirty years of my own suffering and

A DREAM PLAY

others'.

DAUGHTER   It is so heavy...and it stings like nettles!

GATEKEEPER   Well, wear it if you want to...call me when it gets too heavy, and I'll come to relieve you.

DAUGHTER   Good-bye! If you can do it, I should be able to!

GATEKEEPER   We shall see! But be good to all my little friends, and don't grow tired of their complaints.

(She disappears down the alley. The stage becomes pitch-black. When the lights return the lime tree is bare of leaves, the blue monkshood is withered, and the green at the end of the alley has turned brown. The OFFICER enters with grey hair and a grey beard. His clothes are loose-fitting, his collar loose and dirty. Only the stems of his roses are left. He paces up and down.)

OFFICER   It looks as if summer is past, and autumn is coming! Look at that lime tree--and the monkshood! But the autumn is my spring--now they will open the theater again! And then she must come. May I sit on this stool for a while?

DAUGHTER   Sit down, my friend. I can stand for a while.

OFFICER (sitting)   If only I could sleep a little things would be better! (For a moment or two he dozes, then jumps up and resumes his pacing. He stops before the cloverleaf.) This door gives me no peace! What is behind it?...there must be something...

(From the dance floor above faint music is heard.)

Ah! Rehearsals have started!

(The stage is lit by regular flashes, as if from a lighthouse.)

What's that? (Speaking in time with the light.) Light and dark; light and dark.

DAUGHTER (imitating him)   Day and night; day and night. A blessed providence is shortening your wait; and so the days fly by, pursuing the nights!

(The light becomes steady. The BILLSTICKER enters with his fishing net and his tools.)

OFFICER   There's the Billsticker! How was the fishing?

BILLSTICKER   Pretty good! The summer was hot and a bit long; and the net, well, the net was all right, but it wasn't exactly what I had in mind...

OFFICER Not exactly what you had in mind! That's well said; nothing is ever exactly what we had in mind. The idea is always more than the action itself, always more than reality.

(He paces up and down again, and beats the roses against the wall so that the last petals fall off.)

BILLSTICKER Hasn't she come yet?

OFFICER No, not yet; but she'll be here soon. Do you know what's behind that door?

BILLSTICKER No; I've never seen it open.

OFFICER Well, I'm going to call a locksmith to come and open it!

(He goes in to telephone. The BILLSTICKER begins to paste a notice on the billboard.)

DAUGHTER What was the matter with your fishing net?

BILLSTICKER The matter? Well, there wasn't really anything the matter with it...but...well, it wasn't exactly what I had in mind, and so I didn't really enjoy it as much...

DAUGHTER What exactly did you have in mind?

BILLSTICKER Well, that's hard to say...

DAUGHTER Let me tell you. What you had in mind wasn't exactly _that_ one; a green one, but not _that_ green exactly!

BILLSTICKER You understand! You understand everything; that's why everyone brings their problems to you. If you would only listen to me, too, just for once...

DAUGHTER I will; gladly. Come in here and tell me everything.

(She goes into the lodge. BILLSTICKER stands outside talking to her through the window.)

*

(Darkness again. The lime tree blossoms again, as does the monkshood, and the sun shines on the green at the end of the alley. The OFFICER is now old and white-haired, his clothes ragged, his shoes worn out. He carries the stems of the roses. As he paces up and down his gait is that of an old man. He reads the billboard. A BALLET DANCER enters from the right.)

OFFICER Has Miss Victoria gone yet?

A DREAM PLAY

DANCER   No, she hasn't.

OFFICER   Then I'll wait! She'll be here soon, I'm sure.

DANCER   I'm sure she will.

OFFICER   Now don't go! Don't you want to see what's behind that door? I've sent for a locksmith!

DANCER   Oh, I'd really be interested to see that door opened! That door, the growing castle...do you know the growing castle?

OFFICER   Do I! After being a prisoner there for seven years?

DANCER   No! Was that you? But why do they have so many horses there?

OFFICER   Why? Because it's a stable castle, of course!

DANCER (distressed)   Oh how silly I am! I should have known that!

*

(CHORUS GIRL comes in from right.)

OFFICER   Has Miss Victoria gone?

CHORUS GIRL   No, she's not gone. She never goes!

OFFICER   That is because she loves me. You ought not to leave before the smith comes to open this door!

CHORUS GIRL   Oh, is the door to be opened? How exciting! I just want to ask the gatekeeper something!

*

(PROMPTER in from right.)

OFFICER   Has Miss Victoria gone?

PROMPTER   Not as far as I know.

OFFICER   Look! Don't tell her I'm waiting for her. But don't go before this door is opened.

PROMPTER   What door?

OFFICER   Is there more than one door?

PROMPTER   Oh, now I get you; the one with the cloverleaf. I'll certainly stay for that. I just want a word with the gatekeeper.

*

(The DANCER, CHORUS GIRL, and PROMPTER group themselves around the BILLSTICKER outside the GATEKEEPER'S window, and talk to the DAUGHTER in turn. GLAZIER enters from the alley.)

OFFICER   Is that the locksmith?

GLAZIER   No, I'm not a locksmith; he had visitors. But a glazier is just as good.

OFFICER   Of course, of course! But do you have your diamond?

GLAZIER   Naturally! What use is a glazier without his diamond?

OFFICER   None, of course. Well, let's get to work.

(He claps his hands. Everyone gathers in a circle round the door. Chorus Girls dressed for Die Meistersinger, and dancers from Aida wander in from the right.)

*

OFFICER   Smith--or glazier--do your duty!

(The GLAZIER comes forward, diamond in hand.)

A moment such as this seldom returns in a man's life; and so, my friends, I beg you--a few reflections...

*

POLICEMAN   In the name of the law, I forbid you to open that door!

OFFICER   Oh God, what a fuss whenever anyone wants to do something new and great! We'll go to court! Get a lawyer! Then we'll see if this law stands. A lawyer!

*

(The LAWYER'S office. The gateway is now the entrance to an office with a counter running right across the stage. The GATEKEEPER'S room

A DREAM PLAY

is the lawyer's study, the lime tree, without its leaves, is a hat-stand. The billboard is hung with official notices and proclamations. The cloverleaf door is a filing cabinet. The LAWYER is in a frock-coat and white collar. His features bear witness to untold suffering: his face is chalk-white and deeply furrowed, and he has dark blue shadows beneath his eyes. He is ugly, and his face reflects every kind of crime and debt brought to him by his profession. Of his two CLERKS, one has only one arm, the other only one eye. The people gathered to see the opening of the door are still present, but now they have the air of waiting for an appointment, and seem to have been standing there forever. At their head are the DAUGHTER and the OFFICER. The LAWYER approaches the DAUGHTER.)

LAWYER   My dear, may I have that shawl; as soon as I have a fire I will burn it and all its sorrows and miseries.

DAUGHTER   Not yet, my dear brother. First it must be completely full. I want to gather up all your sorrows, all your knowledge of crime and debt, injustice and wrongful imprisonment, slander and libel...

LAWYER   Oh my dear sister, your shawl could never hold them! Look at these walls--you would think all the world's sins had stained that wallpaper. Look at my desk: covered with tales of injustice. And look at me! No one ever comes here to smile: I see only evil looks, bared teeth, clenched fists; and everyone spits evil, envy, and suspicion at me. Look at my cracked and bleeding hands, look at the filth on them; how am I ever to be clean again? I can't even keep my clothes for more than a few days, they stink of crime. Sometimes I disinfect this place with sulphur, but it doesn't help. I have to sleep here, and I dream of nothing but crime... At this very moment I have a murder case before the court. That's bad enough, but do you know the worst thing of all? Divorce! In those cases heaven and earth scream aloud at the betrayal of every primal force, every source of good, the betrayal of love itself. And then, when you've filled reams of paper with their mutual complaints, if you finally take one or other of them aside and lovingly ask them the simple question: what do you really have against your husband or your wife--they stand speechless! They can't give you an answer. Oh yes, once it had something to do with a salad, another time it was about a word--usually it's about nothing at all! But the anguish, the suffering! Those are what I have to bear! Look at me! Could I win a woman's love with this criminal face? Would anyone show me friendship, when I have to enforce society's debts? I tell you, it's wretched to be a human being!

DAUGHTER   Yes, human beings deserve our pity.

LAWYER   True enough! What they live on is a mystery to me! They get married on two thousand a year, when they need four thousand... of course they borrow, they all borrow! They hang on somehow until they die, but they're always in debt. God knows who pays in the end.

DAUGHTER   He who feeds the birds.

LAWYER Yes! But if he who feeds the birds came down to earth to see what life is really like, he would be filled with compassion...

DAUGHTER Human beings need compassion!

LAWYER That's the truth! (To OFFICER.) What do you want?

*

OFFICER I just wanted to ask whether Miss Victoria had gone.

LAWYER No, she hasn't, you can be sure of that. Why do you keep poking at my cabinet?

OFFICER That door seems so like...

LAWYER Oh no, no, no!

(Church bells ring.)

*

OFFICER Is there a funeral somewhere?

LAWYER No, it's graduation day; they're giving out doctor's degrees. As a matter of fact, I'm to be made a Doctor of Law myself. How would you like to come for a degree?

OFFICER Yes, why not? It's one way of passing the time.

LAWYER Then we ought to leave for the ceremony at once. Go and change clothes.

(The OFFICER goes out. Darkness. The office counter now becomes the altar rail of a cathedral, the notice board displays hymn numbers, the coat hanger/lime tree is a candelabra, the LAWYER'S desk a lectern, and the cloverleaf door now leads to the vestry. The CHORUS become ushers, the DANCERS carry laurel wreaths. The rest of the cast are spectators.

At the back is a large organ over whose keyboard hangs a mirror. Music. On each side stand the DEANS OF THE FOUR FACULTIES. For a moment everything freezes. Then USHERS enter from the right, followed by the DANCERS with laurel wreaths in their outstretched hands. From the left three candidates enter, and are crowned with laurel by the DANCERS; they exit right. The LAWYER comes forward to be crowned, but the DANCER turns away in a gesture of refusal, and all the DANCERS leave. Shaken, the LAWYER leans against a pillar. Slowly everyone leaves and the LAWYER is alone.)

*

DAUGHTER (entering, a white shawl over her head and shoulders) Look, I've washed the shawl! But why do you stand like that? Didn't you get your degree?

LAWYER No; I was unworthy.

DAUGHTER Why? Because you defended the poor, found some good in the criminal, eased the penalties for the guilty and found reprieve for the condemned. Pitiful mankind! They are no angels--yet they need pity.

LAWYER Don't speak evil of mankind; I have to plead for them.

DAUGHTER (leaning against the organ) Why do they lash out, even at their friends?

LAWYER Because they know no better.

DAUGHTER Then let us teach them? Will you--you and I?

LAWYER They won't be taught! If only our misery were known to the gods in heaven!

DAUGHTER It shall be! (Sitting at the organ.) Do you know what I can see in this mirror? The world as it ought to be. As it is, it's inside-out.

LAWYER But how did it become that way?

DAUGHTER When the copy was made...

LAWYER That's it! The copy! I always suspected that the copy was faulty...and when I began to realize how things were meant to be I became discontent with everything. People called it cynicism, and told me I had only the vision of the devil...

DAUGHTER Everything is distorted! Look at those four faculties, every one of them supported by society. The theologians teach about God, and the philosophers attack and ridicule their teaching, claiming wisdom only for themselves! Medicine contradicts philosophy, and refuses to acknowledge theology as a science at all, merely superstition...and yet they all sit together in the same council--to teach young people to respect the university! It's simply a madhouse! But God help the first man to become sane!

LAWYER Oh, the theologians are the first to know. They read philosophy as a preliminary study, and learn that theology is nonsense; then they read theology, and learn that philosophy is nonsense. They're mad!

DAUGHTER And the law, serving everyone except its own servants.

LAWYER Justice, even when it tries to do right, is simply man's curse. Justice--which is so often injustice.

DAUGHTER   This is the way you have made it, children of men! Children!--Come, you shall receive a laurel wreath from me...one that will suit you better.

(She places a crown of thorns on his head.)

Now I shall play for you.

(She sits at the organ and plays a Kyrie, but instead of the organ we hear human voices.)

CHILDREN'S VOICES   Lord, Lord! (The last note is held.)

WOMEN'S VOICES   Have mercy upon us! (The last note is held.)

MEN'S VOICES (tenor)   Grant us thy salvation, for thy mercy's sake! (The last note is held.)

MEN'S VOICES (bass)   Save thy children, O Lord, and turn away thine anger from us.

ALL   Have mercy upon us, O Lord, have mercy upon us! Have pity upon men, O Eternal God, and mercifully hear us when we call upon Thee. Out of the deep we cry for grace, O Lord. Let not the burden be too heavy upon us. Hear us, oh Lord, hear us!

*

(The stage slowly darkens. The DAUGHTER rises and approaches the LAWYER. The lighting changes so that the cathedral becomes Fingal's Cave. The waves swell through the basalt pillars, accompanied by the sounds of wind and water.)

LAWYER   Sister, where are we?

DAUGHTER   What do you hear?

LAWYER   I hear waterdrops...

DAUGHTER   Tears, human tears... What else can you hear?

LAWYER   Sighing, moaning, weeping...

DAUGHTER   Human misery has reached this place...to go no further. But why this perpetual misery? Is there nothing in life to be glad about?

LAWYER   Yes, the loveliest thing of all, and the bitterest. Love! A wife and home, the highest and lowest knowledge a man can have!

DAUGHTER Will you let me put that to the test?

LAWYER With me?

DAUGHTER With you! You know the rocks, the stumbling blocks. Let us avoid them!

LAWYER But I am poor!

DAUGHTER What does that matter, if we love one another! A little beauty costs nothing.

LAWYER Perhaps my likes are your dislikes.

DAUGHTER Then we must compromise!

LAWYER What if we become bored with one another?

DAUGHTER Children will come, giving us new pleasure every day!

LAWYER You, you will have me, ugly, despised and rejected by men?

DAUGHTER Yes! Let us unite our destinies!

LAWYER So be it.

(A very simple room in the LAWYER'S office. To the right a large double bed, curtained; by it a window. To the left a stove and kitchen utensils. KRISTIN is pasting lengths of paper inside the window. At the back, an open door to the office. Outside can be seen poor people waiting for interviews with the LAWYER.)

KRISTIN I paste! I paste!

DAUGHTER (pale, worn, sits at the stove) You're shutting out the air! I'm choking!

KRISTIN There's only one small crack left now!

DAUGHTER Air! I can't breathe!

KRISTIN I paste! I paste!

LAWYER That's right, Kristin. Heating is expensive.

DAUGHTER I feel as if you had glued up my mouth!

LAWYER (standing in the doorway) Is the child asleep?

DAUGHTER Yes, at last.

LAWYER (gently) The crying frightens my clients away.

DAUGHTER (amiably)   What can we do about it?

LAWYER   Nothing.

DAUGHTER   We could take a bigger apartment.

LAWYER   We can't afford to.

DAUGHTER   Can I open a window? This bad air is choking me.

LAWYER   Then you let the warmth out, and we'll freeze.

DAUGHTER   It's horrible! Then at least let's scrub this room.

LAWYER   You detest scrubbing, and so do I; and Kristin has to paste. I want the whole house pasted, every crack, the roof, the floors, the walls!

DAUGHTER   I was prepared for poverty, but not for dirt.

LAWYER   Poverty is always more or less dirty.

DAUGHTER   This is worse than I dreamed!

LAWYER   It's not as bad as it could be; we still have food.

DAUGHTER   But what food!

LAWYER   Cabbage is cheap, nourishing, and good.

DAUGHTER   For those who like cabbage! I **can't** bear it!

LAWYER   Why didn't you say so?

DAUGHTER   Because I loved you. I wanted to sacrifice my own tastes.

LAWYER   Then I must sacrifice my taste for cabbage. A sacrifice should be mutual.

DAUGHTER   Then what shall we eat? Fish? But you hate fish.

LAWYER   And it's expensive.

DAUGHTER   This is harder than I thought.

LAWYER (friendly still)   Yes, you see how hard it is; and our child, who should bring us together as a blessing to us...is our undoing.

DAUGHTER   Darling, I am dying in this air, in this room with only a backyard to look at, with the child's screaming for endless sleepless hours, all the people out there complaining and quarreling and accusing each other. I shall die here.

A DREAM PLAY

LAWYER   Poor little flower, without light, without air...

DAUGHTER   And you tell me that things are worse for others...

LAWYER   I am one of the most envied people in the neighborhood.

DAUGHTER   None of it would matter, if I could only find some beauty in this home.

LAWYER   I know you mean a flower, I know you'd like a heliotrope; but that costs one and a half crowns--12 pints of milk and a bushel of potatoes!

DAUGHTER   I would gladly go without food for the sake of a flower.

LAWYER   There is a kind of beauty which costs nothing, and whose absence from the home is a torment to any man with any sense of beauty.

DAUGHTER   What is it?

LAWYER   Oh, if I tell you, you'll be angry.

DAUGHTER   We have agreed not to get angry.

LAWYER   We have agreed... Everything will be all right, Agnes, if we avoid curtness or harshness of speech. You know what I mean? No, perhaps not yet.

DAUGHTER   We should always avoid that.

LAWYER   And we always shall, if it depends on me.

DAUGHTER   So tell me now.

LAWYER   All right. Whenever I enter a room I always look first to see whether the curtains are hung properly. (Goes to curtains and adjusts them.) If they hang down like a rope or an old piece of rag I leave quickly. Then I take a look at the chairs: if they are in their right place I stay. (Moves a chair against the wall.) I check to see that the candles stand straight in the candlesticks, as they should in a well-ordered house. (Adjusts candle.) This is the beauty, my little friend, which costs nothing!

DAUGHTER (bowing her head)   Axel, curt...harsh...

LAWYER   I was not...

DAUGHTER   Yes you were!

LAWYER   For God's sake...

DAUGHTER   What sort of language is that!

LAWYER Forgive me, Agnes. But I have suffered as much from your untidiness as you have suffered from dirt. And I've not dared to tidy things myself in case you were angry, and we quarreled. Shall we stop now?

DAUGHTER It is so hard to be married. Harder than anything. People need to be angels.

LAWYER Yes.

DAUGHTER I think I shall begin to hate you after this!

LAWYER Then God help us! But we can prevent hatred. I give you my word, I will never mention your untidiness again...even though it's a torture for me!

DAUGHTER And I shall eat cabbage, even though it sickens me.

LAWYER So, a life of torment--together! What pleases one of us will torment the other.

DAUGHTER Human life is so pitiful.

LAWYER You see that?

DAUGHTER Yes. But in God's name let us avoid the rocks, now that we know them so well.

LAWYER Yes, we can do that. After all, we're enlightened, humane people. We can obviously forgive one another and make allowances.

DAUGHTER We can even learn to smile at trifles.

LAWYER Yes, at least we can do that... Do you know, I read in the paper this morning...where is the paper?

DAUGHTER (embarrassed) Which paper?

LAWYER (hard) Do we take more than one paper?

DAUGHTER Now smile, don't talk so harshly... I lit the fire with your paper.

LAWYER (violently) The hell you did!

DAUGHTER Smile...I burned it because it mocked what I believe to be holy.

LAWYER And what I believe to be unholy! (Striking his hands together repeatedly.) I'll smile, I'll smile until you can see my back teeth... I'll be humane, and hide my opinions, I'll say yes to everything, I'll cant and I'll cringe. So you have burnt my paper! (Adjusts bedcurtains.) Look at that! Now, let's begin to tidy this place up, and see how you like that!... Agnes, this is quite impossible!

DAUGHTER   I know it.

LAWYER   We must put up with it! Not for the sake of our promises, but for the child.

DAUGHTER   Yes, for the child...

LAWYER   So now I have to meet my clients! Listen, you can hear them already, muttering in impatience to tear one another to pieces, torture one another with fines and imprisonment...the souls of the damned!

DAUGHTER   Poor, poor humanity. Oh, this pasting!

KRISTIN   I paste! I paste!

(LAWYER stands in the doorway and fidgets nervously with the handle.)

DAUGHTER   Oh, how that handle squeals. It's as if my heart were being crushed!

LAWYER   I crush! I crush!

DAUGHTER   Don't do that!

LAWYER   I crush...

DAUGHTER   No!

LAWYER   I...

OFFICER (entering)   Allow me!

*

LAWYER (releasing handle)   Certainly! Since you have your degree!

OFFICER   Yes! Now everything in life is mine, every path is open to me! I have set foot on Parnassus, won my laurels, immortality, honor, everything is mine!

LAWYER   What will you live on?

OFFICER   Live on?

LAWYER   I take it you'd like a home, clothes, food?

OFFICER   You can always find them, if only you have someone to hold on to.

LAWYER Perhaps...perhaps. Paste, Kristin, paste, until they can no longer breathe! (Exits backwards, bowing farewell.)

KRISTIN I paste! I paste! Until they can no longer breathe!

*

OFFICER Are you coming with me now?

DAUGHTER Yes! But where?

OFFICER Fairhaven! To the summer, sunshine, youth, children and flowers, singing and dancing, feasting and joy!

DAUGHTER Then I will come!

OFFICER Come!

*

LAWYER (entering) And I return to my first hell. This was the second... and greatest! The loveliest things in life bring us the greatest damnation. Look at that, hairpins on the floor again! (Picks hairpin from the floor.)

OFFICER Look, now he's discovered the hairpin too!

LAWYER Too?... Look at it: two prongs, but only one pin. If I unbend it...one! Bend it back...two! Yet it never stops being one. But if I break it...so...then there are two! (Breaks hairpin and throws pieces away.)

OFFICER So he understands all that. But before you can break it the prongs must separate. Unless they do that they cannot be broken.

LAWYER But look, they are parallel--they never approach one another, and they neither hold together nor break apart.

OFFICER This hairpin is the most perfect of all created things! One straight line which is two parallel lines.

LAWYER A lock which encloses when it is open.

OFFICER Open, it encloses the loose hair, closed it releases...

LAWYER It's like that door! When I close it, I open the way out for you, Agnes. (Exits, closing the door behind him.)

*

DAUGHTER   And now?

(Scene change: the curtained bed is transformed into a tent. The stove remains. To the right are burnt hills, dotted with stumps of withered heather. Red pigsties and outhouses. In front of them an open space for remedial exercises, where people are exercising on machines resembling instruments of torture. To the left, foreground, part of the quarantine building: open shed with furnaces, boilers, and pipes. In the middle distance, an open bay. On the other side a beautiful shore decked with flags, where white boats are moored, some with sails set, some without. Small Italian villas, pavilions, kiosks, and marble statues visible among the foliage.

The QUARANTINE MASTER, in a black mask, is walking on the beach.)

OFFICER   Why, Gasbag! You here?

Q.M.   Yes, I'm here.

OFFICER   Isn't this Fairhaven?

Q.M.   No, that's on the other side. This is Foulstrand.

OFFICER   Then we've come to the wrong place!

Q.M.   We! Aren't you going to introduce me?

OFFICER   No, that wouldn't be right! (Sotto voice.) After all, she is Indra's daughter.

Q.M.   Indra's daughter? I thought it was Waruna. But aren't you surprised at my black face?

OFFICER   My son, I'm fifty years old; at that age nothing surprises you any more. Anyway, I guessed right away that you were going to a masquerade this afternoon.

Q.M.   Absolutely right! I hope you'll come too?

OFFICER   Certainly...especially as I don't much like the look of this place. What sort of people live here?

Q.M.   Everyone here is sick; the healthy ones live over there!

OFFICER   You mean that only poor people live here?

Q.M.   Good God no! These are the rich! Look at that fellow lying on the rack: he's had too much paté de foie gras and truffles, and guzzled too much Burgundy; now he's got knotted feet!

OFFICER   Knotted feet?

Q.M.   Sure! His feet are all twisted up! You see that fellow on the guillotine? He's drunk so much brandy that we've got to crush his backbone!

OFFICER   Not exactly pleasant, either...

Q.M.   Everyone here has some misery or other to hide. Take a look at him, for example.

(An aging DANDY is pushed on in a wheelchair, accompanied by a thin, ugly sixty-year-old COQUETTE, dressed in the latest fashion, and escorted by a "FRIEND" of about forty.)

OFFICER   That's the Major! Our old schoolmate!

Q.M.   Don Juan! Look at that--he's still in love with the old spook at his side! He can't see that she's aged, ugly, cruel, and unfaithful.

OFFICER   Ah, true love! I never thought that flighty old rake had it in him to love so deeply and seriously.

Q.M.   That's a nice way of putting it, I must say!

OFFICER   Oh, I've been in love myself...with Victoria! I still pace up and down that corridor waiting for her.

Q.M.   Hey! Are you the chap who walks up and down the corridor?

OFFICER   Yes, I'm the one.

Q.M.   Tell me, have you opened that door yet?

OFFICER   No, the court's still considering the case. The trouble is that the Billsticker went off for a fishing holiday, so his evidence has been delayed. Still, while we're waiting I've got the glazier to put new windows in the castle. It's grown half a new wing, you know; but it's been an unusually good year, warm and muggy.

Q.M.   You can bet that you haven't been as warm as they have! (Pointing to residents.)

OFFICER   Why, how hot are those ovens?

Q.M.   When we're disinfecting cholera suspects, 140 degrees.

OFFICER   Another cholera epidemic?

Q.M.   Didn't you know that?

OFFICER   Well,...of course I knew it...but I often forget what I know.

Q.M.   I wish I could forget things...most of all, myself. That's why I keep an eye open for masquerades, fancy-dress, or theatricals.

A DREAM PLAY

OFFICER   Why, what happened to you?

Q.M.   If I talk about it people say I'm bragging; if I keep it quiet they call me a damned hypocrite.

OFFICER   Is that why you've blackened your face?

Q.M.   Yes; it's just a shade blacker than I *am*!

OFFICER   Who's this?

Q.M.   Oh, him; he's a poet. He's come for his mudbath!

(The POET enters, gazing at the sky, and carrying a bucket of mud.)

OFFICER   Jesus, a poet ought to bathe in the light and in the air!

Q.M.   No; he spends so much time in higher realms that he feels a longing to get back to the mud. It toughens his hide, just as it does for pigs wallowing in the mire! He can't feel the gadflies stinging after that.

OFFICER   What a strange world of contradictions!

*

POET (ecstatic)   Out of clay the god Ptah created mankind, on a potter's wheel, a lathe,...(Cynical.) or whatever the hell it was!... (Ecstatic.) Of clay the sculptor creates his more or less immortal masterpieces... (Cynical.) which are usually sheer junk! (Ecstatic.) From clay are created those receptacles so necessary for the pantry, whose common names are pots, plates...(Cynical.) as if I gave a fiddler's damn what they are called! (Ecstatic.) This, this is clay! And when clay is thinned, we have...*mud*! (Calling.) Lina!

*

(Enter LINA with a bucket.)

POET   Lina, show yourself to Miss Agnes. She knew you ten years ago, when you were young, happy, and even, let us say, a beautiful girl... Now look at her! Five children, drudgery, screaming, starving, and beating! See how that beauty has gone, how happiness has disappeared--all through the exercise of duties, which should have given that inner satisfaction seen in the still harmony of a face or the quiet glow in the eyes.

Q.M. (putting his hand over the POET'S mouth)   Hold your tongue! Hold your tongue!

POET That's what everyone says! And if you shut your mouth, they shout: Speak! People are so inconsistent.

*

DAUGHTER (to LINA) Tell me your grievances.

LINA No, I daren't! It would only make things worse.

DAUGHTER Who can be so cruel to you?

LINA I don't dare talk about it. I'd be beaten.

POET That may be so; but I'll tell you, even if that blackamoor knocks the teeth out of my head! I'll tell you that life is unjust! Agnes, daughter of the gods: can you hear music and dancing up on that hill? Well, that's for Lina's sister. She's come home from the city, where she ran completely wild, you know what I mean. Now she's back, and they're slaughtering the fatted calf; but Lina, who stayed at home, has to pick up that pail and feed the pigs.

DAUGHTER But they're not celebrating a sister's return home, but her salvation from an evil way of life; you should understand that.

POET Then let them arrange dances and dinners every night, to honor this blameless servant, who never took a false path. Let's see them do that! But do they? When Lina's free she's told to go to her prayers, and is blamed for not being perfect. Is that justice?

DAUGHTER Your questions are so hard to answer, because...because there are so many unforeseen circumstances...

POET The Caliph Harun the Just could see that, too. He sat up there on his throne and never saw what things were like down here. Then one fine day, at last!, complaints reached even his lofty ears. He came down here, disguised himself, and went unrecognized among the people to see how awful justice could be!

DAUGHTER Surely you don't think that I'm Harun the Just.

OFFICER Let's talk about something else!... People are coming...

(A white, dragon-shaped boat, with blue silken sails and a golden mast with rose-red pennants glides into the sound from the left. At the helm sit HE and SHE, their arms around one another.)

OFFICER Look at that: perfect happiness, bliss beyond measure, the joy of young love!

(The stage brightens.)

*

A DREAM PLAY

HE (standing in the boat and singing)
    Greetings, fair bay,
    In the springtime of my youth
    Here I dreamed my first rosy dreams,
    And here I return,
    No longer alone!
    Forests and bays,
    Heavens and sea,
    Greet her!
    My love, my bride,
    My sun, my life!

(They are greeted by the Fairhaven flags, white handkerchiefs waving from villas and shores, and the harmony of harps and violins echoing over the bay.)

POET   See how radiant they are. Listen to the echoes across the bay. Love!

OFFICER   That is Victoria!

Q.M.   Well, even so...

OFFICER   She is his Victoria, just as I have a Victoria of my own! And no one may see her! Hoist the quarantine-flag, while I pull the catch to shore.

(The QUARANTINE-MASTER waves a golden flag, while the OFFICER pulls the boat to shore on a line.)

Hold on there!

(HE and SHE notice the landscape in horror.)

Q.M.   Yes, I know it's hard, but everyone who comes from a source of infection has to land here.

POET   How can he talk that way, or do such things, when two young people are in love! Leave them alone! Don't meddle with love! It's sacrilege. Now everything beautiful will be dragged down into the mud.

(HE and SHE step ashore, sorrowful and ashamed.)

HE   What have we done?

Q.M.   Done? You don't have to do anything to meet with life's little misfortunes!

SHE   So short are joy and happiness!

HE   How long must we stay here?

Q.M.   Forty days and forty nights.

SHE   We'd rather drown in the sea!

HE   Live here, among burnt hills and pigsties!

POET   Love conquers everything, even sulphur fumes and carbolic acid!

*

Q.M. (lighting the furnace amid clouds of smoke)   There; that's got the sulphur going. Please step inside!

SHE   Oh, my blue dress will lose its color!

Q.M.   White! And your roses will be white too!

HE   And your cheeks! Forty days!

SHE (to OFFICER)   I suppose that pleases you!

OFFICER   No it won't... It's perfectly true that your happiness was the source of my grief, but...it doesn't matter... Now I have my doctor's degree and have a job over there. Well, well! This fall I can get a job in a school somewhere...among little boys, reading the same lessons I read all through my childhood, all through my youth, the same lessons! And they went on, the same things throughout life and into my old age! What is two times two? How many times will two go into four? On it goes, until I can retire--with nothing to do but wait for mealtimes and the newspapers, until they carry me off to the crematorium and burn me to bits. Do you have any retired people here? That's the worst thing in life, except the two-times table: beginning all over again, even after you've graduated; asking the same questions until you die.

(An elderly man strolls by, hands behind his back.)

Look, there goes a pensioner now, waiting for death. No doubt a captain who never got his promotion, or a court clerk who never became a judge; many are called but few are chosen! Look at him, walking around, nothing to do but wait for breakfast...

PENSIONER   No, the paper, the morning paper!

OFFICER   And he's only 54! He's good for another twenty-five years of waiting for meals and papers. Gruesome!

PENSIONER   Tell me something that isn't gruesome! Tell me, tell me, tell me!

OFFICER Yes, tell him, anyone who can! I can't! I've got to sit with little boys and go through the two-times table. How many times does two go into four? (Holds his head in his hands in despair.) And Victoria, whom I loved, for whom I wished the greatest happiness in the world... Now she has happiness, while I suffer...suffer, suffer!

*

SHE Do you think I can be happy when I see your suffering? How can you believe that? Does it make you feel better to know that for forty days and nights I shall be a prisoner here? Does that ease your pain?

OFFICER Yes, and No! Oh, I can enjoy nothing while you are in pain.

HE Can you believe that my happiness could be founded upon your misery?

OFFICER God help us all, all!

ALL (stretching their hands towards heaven and giving a cry of agony like a dissonant chord) Oh!

DAUGHTER Eternal one, hear them! Life is evil! Men deserve your compassion!

ALL (as before) Oh!

*

(Stage darkens. Everything changes place. Foulstrand is now the distant shore and is covered in shadow. Fairhaven lies in the foreground. To the right the corner of a hotel with open windows; dancers can be seen within. On a box outside the hotel stand three maidservants, arms around one another's waists, looking at the dancers. On the steps in front of the building is a bench on which sits UGLY EDITH, bareheaded, unhappy, with long untidy hair. In front of her an open piano. Right, a yellow wooden summerhouse.

Two children, lightly dressed, playing ball.

In the foreground a jetty with white boats, flagstaffs, and flags. In the bay is a white warship, anchored, with guns. The whole landscape is covered with snow, and the trees are bare. Enter DAUGHTER and OFFICER.)

*

DAUGHTER Oh, peace, happiness, holiday time! Work is over, and every day is a feast day. People are in their best clothes, music and dancing even before dinner. (To MAIDS.) Why don't you go in and dance, children?

MAIDS Us?

OFFICER They're servants!

DAUGHTER Of course!... But why should Edith just sit there, instead of dancing?

(EDITH hides her face in her hands.)

OFFICER Don't ask her! She's sat there for three hours without being asked to dance! (He walks into the yellow house.)

DAUGHTER What a cruel pleasure!

*

MOTHER (to EDITH) Why don't you go in, as I told you?

EDITH Because...no one will ask me to dance. I know I'm ugly, and no one wants to dance with me, but I can't bear to be reminded of it all the time!

(She begins to play Bach's Toccata and Fugue number 10. The waltz is heard from the dance-hall, faintly at first but then louder, as if competing with the Bach. EDITH plays it down, and reduces it to silence. The guests are seen listening to her through the doorway; everyone stands solemnly as she plays. A NAVAL OFFICER seizes ALICE, one of the guests, about the waist and leads her towards the jetty.)

NAVAL OFFICER Come, quickly!

(EDITH interrupts her playing, rises, and stares at them in bewilderment. She remains there, frozen.)

*

(The wall to the yellow house is removed. Three boys are sitting in their desks; with them is the OFFICER, looking unhappy and ill at ease. A SCHOOLMASTER with glasses, chalk, and cane, stands in front of them.)

MASTER (to OFFICER) Now my boy, what is two times two?

(OFFICER remains sitting; struggles with difficulty to find the answer.)

A DREAM PLAY

Stand up when you're spoken to!

OFFICER (standing)   Two...times two... Let me see... Two!

MASTER   I see! You have not prepared your lesson.

OFFICER (ashamed)   Yes, I have, but...I know what it is, but I can't say it...

MASTER   You're trying to wriggle out of it! You know it, but you can't say it. Perhaps I can help you. (Pulls OFFICER'S hair.)

OFFICER   Oh that's terrible, terrible!

MASTER   Yes, it's terrible to see such a big boy without ambition.

OFFICER   A big boy; yes I am big, much bigger than the others; I'm grown up, I've finished school...(As if waking.) I've even got my doctor's degree. So why am I sitting here? Haven't I graduated?

MASTER   Oh yes, of course, but you have to stay here until you're mature. Isn't that right?

OFFICER   Yes, of course, one has to mature. Two times two...is two; and I'll prove it by analogy, the highest kind of proof! Listen: One times one is one; therefore two times two is two! After all, what applies in the first case must be true of the second!

MASTER   Your proof is perfectly in accord with the laws of logic, but the answer is wrong!

OFFICER   It can't be wrong if it's logical! Let's go further. One into one is one, therefore two into two is two!

MASTER   Perfectly correct, according to your analogy. But how much is one times three?

OFFICER   Three!

MASTER   Consequently two times three is three too?

OFFICER (thoughtful)   No, that can't be right...it can't. Otherwise... (Baffled.) No, no, I'm not mature yet!

MASTER   No, you're not nearly mature yet.

OFFICER   How long have I got to sit here then?

MASTER   How long? Here? Do you really think time and space exist? But let's suppose that time does exist: if so, we ought to be able to say what it is. What is time?

OFFICER   Time... I can't say it, but I know what it is. Therefore

I can know what two times two is, even though I can't say it! Can
you tell us what time is?

MASTER   Of course I can!

ALL   Tell us then.

MASTER   Time... Let me see. (Stands worriedly with his finger to
his nose.) While we are talking time flies. Thus, time is something
which flies while I talk!

BOY   He's talking now; and while he's talking I'm going to fly.
Therefore I am time! (Flies.)

MASTER   That's perfectly correct, according to the laws of logic.

OFFICER   Then the laws of logic are crazy, because Nils can't be
time!

MASTER   That is also correct according to the laws of logic, even
though it's crazy.

OFFICER   Then logic is crazy!

MASTER   It certainly looks that way. But if logic is crazy, then
the whole world is crazy...and I'm damned if I'm going to stay here
and teach a pile of nonsense. If someone will stand us a drink we
could go for a swim.

OFFICER   That's a posterius prius, a topsy-turvy world. You usually
swim first and drink afterwards. Old fool!

MASTER   You should not be conceited, Doctor!

OFFICER   Captain, if you don't mind! Yes, I am a Captain, and I
don't see why I should sit here and be insulted among a bunch of
kids.

MASTER   (raising a finger)   We must mature!

*

Q.M. (entering)   The quarantine's beginning!

OFFICER   So there you are! Can you believe it, that fellow made
me sit at a desk, even though I've graduated!

Q.M.   Why didn't you just get up and go?

OFFICER   Go?...that's not so easy!

A DREAM PLAY

MASTER   I thought not! Try!

OFFICER (to Q.M.)   Save me! I can't stand those eyes!

Q.M.   Oh come on; come and join in the dancing. We have to dance before the infection breaks out. We must!

OFFICER   Is the ship leaving?

Q.M.   Yes, almost at once. There'll be plenty of tears shed then.

OFFICER   Always tears! When we come and when we go. Come on.

(They leave. The MASTER silently continues his class.)

*

(The MAIDS who have been standing by the window of the dance hall draw sadly towards the harbor. EDITH, who has been frozen beside the piano, follows them.)

DAUGHTER (to OFFICER)   Aren't there any happy people in this paradise?

OFFICER   Of course. There are two newlyweds. Listen to them.

*

HUSBAND   My happiness is so boundless that I could die.

WIFE   Die? What for?

HUSBAND   Because in the midst of happiness grows the seed of unhappiness; it consumes itself like fire. Nothing can burn forever, and extinction is bound to come sooner or later. This foreknowledge of the end destroys happiness at its supreme moment.

WIFE   Then let us die together, now!

HUSBAND   Die? Yes. I am afraid of happiness, the deceiver!

(They walk towards the sea.)

*

DAUGHTER   Life is evil! Men are to be pitied.

OFFICER   Then look at this fellow. He's the most envied person here.

He owns hundreds of Italian villas, all these bays, beaches, woods, the fish in the water, the birds in the air, and the game in the woods. He has thousands of tenants, and the sun rises over his water and sets over his land.

DAUGHTER   Does he complain too?

OFFICER   Yes, and with reason. He cannot see.

Q.M.   He's blind.

DAUGHTER   And the most envied!

OFFICER   He's come to say good-bye to his son, who is on that ship.

*

BLIND MAN   I cannot see, but I can hear! I can hear the anchor tearing at the sea-bed like a hook tearing at the guts of a fish. My son, my only child, traveling to a strange land across the sea! And I can go with him only in my thoughts. There's the cable rattling, and...something...is flapping and lashing like wet clothes on a line... wet handkerchiefs perhaps...and sighing and sniffing as if people were weeping...could be small waves lapping the boards or some deserted girl crying on shore...abandoned...faithless... I asked a child once why the sea was salt, and the child, whose father was faraway at sea, answered at once: because the sailors cry so much. And why should they cry? Because they are always going away, and their handkerchiefs are hung from the masts to dry. Why should a man weep when he is unhappy? I asked. Oh, he said, because the eye should be washed sometimes, so that we can see more clearly.

(The ship raises sail and sails away; the girls on the shore wave their handkerchiefs and dry their eyes by turn. From the foremast a signal is raised: "Yes"--a red ball on a white background. ALICE waves jubilantly in answer.)

DAUGHTER   What does that flag mean?

OFFICER   It means "Yes"; it's the lieutenant's "yes" in red, like red heart's blood, written on the blue of the sky.

DAUGHTER   What's the sign for "No" then?

OFFICER   Blue, like poisoned blood in blue veins...but look how happy Alice is.

DAUGHTER   And look how Edith weeps.

BLIND MAN   Meet and part! Meet and part! Such is life. I met his mother; and she went. I still had a son; and now he's gone.

A DREAM PLAY

DAUGHTER   But he'll come back again...

BLIND MAN   Who is that? I have heard that voice before, in my dreams, in my youth, when summer holidays began, and in the earliest days of my marriage, when my son was born; every time life smiled on me I heard that voice, like the south wind, or a harmony of harps above my head, as if I imagined the angels' greeting on the first Christmas night.

*

(LAWYER enters and whispers to BLIND MAN.)

BLIND MAN   Indeed!

LAWYER   Yes, it's the truth! (To DAUGHTER.) You have seen most things now, but you've still not seen the worst.

DAUGHTER   Can anything be worse?

LAWYER   Repetition, reiterations, going back! Learning all the old lessons again. Come with me.

DAUGHTER   Where?

LAWYER   To your duties!

DAUGHTER   Duties! What are they?

LAWYER   Everything you most detest! All the things you don't want to do but must. Abstentions, renunciations, evasions, departures... everything disagreeable or repulsive or painful.

DAUGHTER   But are there no pleasant duties?

LAWYER   They are pleasant only when they are fulfilled.

DAUGHTER   When they no longer exist! If duty is everything unpleasant, what is there that is pleasant?

LAWYER   Anything pleasant is a sin!

DAUGHTER   Sin?

LAWYER   And sin must be punished! Every time I have enjoyed a day or an evening I've been tormented like hell with an evil conscience.

DAUGHTER   Strange!

LAWYER   I wake in the mornings with a headache; and then the repetition begins, that twisted repetition. Everything that had been beautiful the night before, everything witty or charming, now comes back as something ugly or repulsive or stupid. Every pleasure rots like that, every joy disintegrates. What people call success is always the cause of the next defeat. Every success I have had in life has turned rotten, because you see, people have an instinctive loathing for other people's good fortune: they think it's unjust of fate to favor one person and not another, and they try to restore the balance by putting obstacles in his way. It's a dangerous thing to have talent-- a man can starve that way! Nonetheless, if you don't go back to your duties I shall bring an action against you and pursue you through the courts!

DAUGHTER Go back? To the stove and the cabbage, the child's clothes...

LAWYER Yes, and there's washing to be done; all the handkerchiefs need washing...

DAUGHTER Must I live through that again?

LAWYER That's all there is in life. Look at that schoolmaster in there...yesterday he graduated, was crowned with a laurel wreath and had the cannons fired in his honor, he trod Parnassus and was embraced by the king!... And now he's back in school again, asking how much is two times two! And he'll stay there until he's dead! So--come back, to your home!

DAUGHTER I would rather die!

LAWYER Die? People can't do that! In the first place, it's such a disgrace that even your corpse would be dishonored; and secondly... you would be damned; it's a mortal sin.

DAUGHTER It's not easy to be a human being.

*

ALL Right!

*

DAUGHTER I will not return to dirt and humiliation with you. I shall go back where I came from, but...first I want to see that door opened and know its secret... I want that door opened!

LAWYER Then you must retrace your old steps, go back the way you have come, withstand all the horrors of a lawsuit, the repetitions, redraftings, reiterations...

DAUGHTER That may be so; but first I am going into the wilderness

A DREAM PLAY

and desolation to find myself again. We shall meet again. (To POET.) Come with me.

(Cries of distress from the distance.)

What was that?

LAWYER The damned souls at Foulstrand.

DAUGHTER But why are they shrieking more than usual today?

LAWYER Because the sun is shining here, because we have music, dancing, youth. They feel their own suffering all the more deeply.

DAUGHTER We must free them!

LAWYER Try! Someone came to free them once, and they hanged him on a cross!

DAUGHTER Who hanged him?

LAWYER All the respectable people.

DAUGHTER And who are they?

LAWYER Don't you know the respectable people? You will!

DAUGHTER Are they the ones who blocked your graduation?

LAWYER Yes.

DAUGHTER Then I know them.

*

(A Mediterranean beach. In the left foreground, a white wall, over which orange trees laden with fruit can be seen. At the back, villas, and the terrace of the Casino. To the right a huge heap of coal and two wheelbarrows. In the distance, to the right, a glimpse of the blue sea.

Two COALHEAVERS, naked to the waist, blackened faces, hands, and bodies, sit despondently beside one of the wheelbarrows.)

DAUGHTER This is paradise!

COALHEAVER I This is hell!

COALHEAVER II 120 degrees in the shade.

COALHEAVER I Let's take a swim.

COALHEAVER II   The police will come. You can't bathe here.

COALHEAVER I   Could we take an orange from that tree?

COALHEAVER II   No, the police would come.

COALHEAVER I   Well, I can't work in this heat; I'm getting out of here.

COALHEAVER II   Then the police will arrest you. (Pause.) Besides, you've got to have food.

COALHEAVER I   Food? We work the most and get the least to eat; and the rich, who do nothing, get the most. You could almost say it's unjust. What does the daughter of the gods say about it?

*

DAUGHTER   I can't answer... What have you done, to be blackened so, and have to work so hard?

COALHEAVER I   Done? We were born of poor and often bad parents. Perhaps been to jail a few times.

DAUGHTER   Jail?

COALHEAVER I   Sure. But all the other guilty ones are sitting up there wining and dining in the Casino.

DAUGHTER (to LAWYER)   Can this be true?

LAWYER   More or less, yes.

DAUGHTER   Do you mean that at some time or another everyone deserves to be sent to prison?

LAWYER   Yes.

DAUGHTER   Even you?

LAWYER   Yes!

DAUGHTER   Is it true that they can't bathe in the sea here?

*

LAWYER   Yes; not even with their clothes on. The only ones who can avoid paying are the ones who try to drown themselves. And they usually get beaten up in the police station.

A DREAM PLAY

DAUGHTER Couldn't they go outside the town and bathe, somewhere in the country?

LAWYER It's all private.

DAUGHTER But I mean out where it's free.

LAWYER Nothing's free. It's all private.

DAUGHTER The sea, the great wide...

LAWYER Private! Everything. You can't sail a boat at sea or bring it to land without registering it and paying for it. A beautiful system!

DAUGHTER This is no paradise!

LAWYER I can promise you that!

DAUGHTER But why don't people do something to improve their situation?

LAWYER Oh, they try; but every time they try someone sends them to prison or the madhouse.

DAUGHTER Who could do that?

LAWYER The respectable people, the honorable...

DAUGHTER But the madhouse...?

LAWYER Their own bewilderment when they see the hopelessness of every effort.

DAUGHTER Hasn't anyone ever considered that there might be some secret reason behind it all?

LAWYER Of course. People who are well off always say that!

DAUGHTER That things are right as they are...

*

COALHEAVER I And yet we're the foundation of society. If we don't get the coal, out goes your stove, your heat, your light, the factories, shops, home; nothing but cold and darkness. We sweat like hell to get the filthy stuff; what do we get in return?

LAWYER Help them. (Pause.) I can see that things can't be the same for everyone, but why such enormous differences?

(MAN and WOMAN walk across the stage.)

*

WOMAN   Are you coming to play cards?

MAN   No, I'd better take a little walk to get an appetite for dinner.

*

COALHEAVER I   To _get_ an appetite!

COALHEAVER II   To _get_...?

(Children rush in, and scream with terror at the sight of the COALHEAVERS

*

COALHEAVER I   They scream at the very sight of us! They scream...

COALHEAVER II   Goddamn! We might as well get the scaffold at once and let these rotten bodies swing!

COALHEAVER I   Goddamn! Goddamn!

*

LAWYER (to DAUGHTER)   It's crazy enough! It's not that people are really so bad, but...

DAUGHTER   But?

LAWYER   The system...

DAUGHTER (hiding her face)   This is no paradise.

COALHEAVERS   No, this is hell!

(Fingal's Cave. A long green swell coming slowly into the cave. In the foreground rides a red buoy, soundless. The music of the waves and the wind.

POET   Where have you brought me?

DAUGHTER   Far from the suffering and mourning of humanity, to the end of the world, to the cave we call Indra's Ear; here the queen of heaven is said to listen to the complaints of men.

POET   What! Here?

DAUGHTER   Can't you see that the cave is built like a shell? Yes,

A DREAM PLAY

you can see it; and you know perfectly well that your ear is built like a shell too. And yet you've never thought about it. (She lifts a shell from the shore.) When you were a child did you ever hold a shell to your ear, to hear the rushing of your heart's blood, the humming of the thoughts in your brain, the breaking-up of thousands of little worn-out threads in the tissues of your body? All this in a tiny little shell! Imagine what can be heard in this great one!

POET   I can hear nothing but the sighing of the wind.

DAUGHTER   Then I will be your interpreter. Listen. The wind's complaint. (Recites to soft music.)

>   Born beneath the skies of heaven,
>   Pursued by Indra's fires,
>   Down to the dusty earth...
>   In the fields our feet were soiled with dust,
>   On the highways our feet were soiled with dust,
>   In the cities our lungs were soiled with smoke,
>   And we had to bear foul vapors and the smells of food and wine.
>   We reached to the wide seas to air our lungs,
>   To shake our wings, and wash our feet.
>   Indra, God of Heaven, hear us! Hear our sighing!
>   The earth is unclean, life is not good,
>   Man neither good nor evil,
>   Men live as they can, one day at a time,
>   Children of dust they wander in dust,
>   Born of the dust they return to the dust,
>   Wingless, they trudge through this world
>   And become soiled by the dust.
>   Is the fault theirs, or yours?

*

POET   I heard once...

DAUGHTER   Hush! The winds are still singing.

>   We, the winds, children of the air,
>   Bear the complaints of men. You heard us
>   In the stovepipe on autumn evenings,
>   In the flues of the oven and in the window cracks,
>   When the rain wept outside on the rooftops,
>   Or on winter evenings in the snowy pine-woods,
>   Over the windy sea you heard us complaining and wailing,
>   In sails and in rigging,
>   We, the winds, the children of the air,
>   Piercing the human breast, learning the music of their anguish,
>   In the sickroom or the battlefield, and mostly in the nursery,
>   Where the newborn suffer, shrieking and bewailing
>   The pain of being alive.

> We, the winds, who whine and whistle,
> Woe, woe, woe!

*

POET   Somewhere before I...

DAUGHTER   Hush! The waves are singing!

> We, the waves, who rock the winds to rest!
> Green waves, wet and salt, like the firewood logs,
> Quenching, burning, washing, bathing,
> Breeding, multiplying. We the waves,
> Who rock the winds to rest!

*

DAUGHTER   False waves, and faithless. Everything on earth is either burned or drowned--in these waves. Look. Look at everything the sea has robbed and crushed. So many ships sunk, and only the figureheads remain! And the names...Justice, Friendship, Golden Peace, Hope--this is all that remains of Hope, treacherous Hope! Spars, oarlocks, bailers. And look: the lifebelt; it saved itself, but abandoned the needy.

POET   The Justice's nameplate is here. That's the one that sailed from Fairhaven with the Blind Man's son aboard. So that sank too! Along with Alice's fiancé, Edith's hopeless love.

DAUGHTER   Blind Man? Fairhaven? I must have dreamed of them! And Alice's fiancé, ugly Edith, Foulstrand, the quarantine, the sulphur and carbolic, graduation in the cathedral, the lawyer's office, Victoria and the corridor, the growing castle and the Officer, I have dreamed it all...

POET   And I have made a poem of it!

DAUGHTER   Then you know what a poem is...

POET   Then you know what a dream is... What is a poem?

DAUGHTER   Not reality, but more than reality, not a dream, but waking dreams...

POET   And the children of men believe that we poets merely play with words...hide and seek!

DAUGHTER   It is just as well, my friend, or the world would be laid waste for lack of encouragement! Everyone would lie on their backs

A DREAM PLAY   101

and stare at the sky; no one would use the plough or the spade, the plane or the ax.

POET   You say this, you, Indra's daughter, child of the heavens?

DAUGHTER   You are right to reproach me. I have been here too long, and like you I have bathed in the mud. My thoughts have mud on their wings and cannot fly, I have earth on my feet and my self. (Lifts her arms.) I am sinking, sinking... Help me Father, God of Heaven! (Silence.) I can no longer hear his answer. No sound from his lips borne by eternity to my ear's shell. The silver thread is broken; I am earthbound!

POET   Are you going to leave us? Soon?

DAUGHTER   As soon as I have burned this dust from my feet; for the sea's waters cannot cleanse me. Why do you ask?

POET   I have a prayer...a petition.

DAUGHTER   What sort of petition?

POET   A petition from men to the ruler of the world, drawn up by a dreamer.

DAUGHTER   To be delivered...?

POET   By Indra's daughter.

DAUGHTER   Can you read me your poem?

POET   I can.

DAUGHTER   Then read it.

POET   It is better for you to read it.

DAUGHTER   Where?

POET   In my thoughts, or here.

(She receives the paper, but reads without it.)

*

DAUGHTER   Well, I will read it.

> Why were you born in pain,
> Why did you torture your mother,
> Human child, when you should bring her

> Mother's joy?
> Why do you waken to life greeting the light
> With a cry of evil and pain?
> Why do you not smile at life, Human child,
> When life's gift should be a joy in itself?
> Why are we born like animals, children of the gods
> And of men?
> The spirit wished some other clothing than this
> Of blood and dirt! Shall God's image cut its teeth...

Enough! The work should not question its creator! No one has solved life's riddle yet!

> And so our wandering course begins,
> Over thorns, thistles, stones;
> If at any time we tread the trodden road
> At once we find that road forbidden;
> If we pluck a flower we find it owned already by another;
> The way across the meadow is closed, and to go forward on your
>   journey
> You must trample another's crops beneath your feet;
> Then others will trample yours, to make the difference less.
> Every pleasure you enjoy brings sorrow to all others,
> But your sorrow brings happiness to none,
> Sorrow always following sorrow!
> So the journey lasts until your death,
> From which another takes his life.

Is it thus, O son of dust, that you aim to reach the light?

POET   How should a son of dust find words, light, clean, and airy enough to step beyond the earth... Child of the gods, translate our sorrows into a tongue which they will understand.

DAUGHTER   I will!

POET (noticing the buoy)   What's that floating there? A buoy?

DAUGHTER   Yes.

POET   It looks like a lung and a windpipe.

DAUGHTER   It's the guardian of the seas, singing when danger is close.

POET   It seems to me that the sea is rising, the waves are higher.

DAUGHTER   You are right.

POET   Look, what's that? A ship, outside the reef!

DAUGHTER   What is it?

POET   The Flying Dutchman!

A DREAM PLAY

DAUGHTER That one! Why is he punished so severely? Why can he never go ashore.

POET Because he had seven unfaithful wives.

DAUGHTER Is he to be punished for that?

POET Yes; he was condemned by the respectable people.

DAUGHTER Strange world! How can he be freed from his curse?

POET Freed? You'd have to be careful about freeing him.

DAUGHTER Why?

POET Because, because...no, it's not the Dutchman! It's an ordinary ship in distress! Why doesn't that buoy sound now? Look, the sea's getting higher, we'll soon be stranded in the cave. There's the ship's bell ringing--we'll have another figurehead here soon! Shriek, buoy, guardian, do your duty!

(The buoy sounds like a foghorn.)

The crew is waving to us...but we...we're lost!

DAUGHTER Don't you want to be saved?

POET Yes, yes of course I do, but not now--and not in the water.

*

CREW (four-part harmony) Kyrie!

POET They're all screaming; and the sea's creaming. But no one listens!

CREW (as before) Kyrie!

DAUGHTER Someone is coming! Who is it?

POET Walking on the water? There's only one man who walks on water; and it's not Peter, the rock, because he sank like a stone.

(A strong white light is seen out at sea.)

CREW (as before) Kyrie!

DAUGHTER Is it Him?

POET The Crucified One!

DAUGHTER   Why was he crucified?

POET   Because he wanted to save...

DAUGHTER   Who--I have forgotten--who crucified him?

POET   Respectable people!

DAUGHTER   What a strange world!

POET   The sea's getting up. It's growing dark. The storm's rising.

*

(Screams of terror from the CREW.)

POET   They're screaming in terror,...when they see their savior. And now...they're jumping overboard, they're afraid of him!

(More screaming from the CREW.)

And now they're screaming because they're going to die! They scream when they're born and scream when they die!

(The waves threaten to overwhelm those in the cave.)

DAUGHTER   If only I were certain that this really is a ship...

POET   To tell the truth...I don't think it is a ship..it's a two-story house with trees around it...and...a telephone pole...a Tower of Babel with its wires stretched to the heavens...to tell the gods...

DAUGHTER   Child, human thoughts need no wires to reach heaven...the prayers of the innocent will traverse the universe. That is no Tower of Babel. If you wish to storm heaven, storm it with your prayers.

POET   No, it's not a house,...not a telephone tower...can you see it?

DAUGHTER   What do you see?

POET   A snow-covered heath, a parade-ground, the winter sun shining behind a church on the hill, and the long shadow of the tower on the snow... Here comes a column of soldiers marching over the heath; they're marching on the tower, up the spire; now they have reached the cross, and...I know the first man to tread on that cross will die! They're getting closer... That corporal in the lead! Ah! A cloud has crossed the heath covering the sun...it's all gone! The water in the cloud quenched the sun's fire! The sun's light created the shadow of the tower, and the cloud's shadow has smothered it...

(During this speech the scene has changed to the theater alley.)

DAUGHTER (to GATEKEEPER) Has the Lord Chancellor come yet?

GATEKEEPER No!

DAUGHTER And the four Deans?

GATEKEEPER No!

DAUGHTER Call them at once; the door must be opened.

GATEKEEPER Is it so urgent?

DAUGHTER Yes! The riddle of the world is said to lie behind that door. Call the Lord Chancellor and the Deans of the Four Faculties!

(GATEKEEPER blows a whistle.)

And don't forget the Glazier and his diamond; we can do nothing without him!

*

OFFICER (enters from back in frock-coat and top hat, a bouquet of roses in his hand; radiantly happy) Victoria!

GATEKEEPER The lady will be here directly.

OFFICER Good! The carriage is waiting, the table is set, the champagne is on ice... May I embrace you Madame. (Embraces GATEKEEPER.) Victoria!

*

WOMAN'S VOICE (above, singing) I am here!

OFFICER (beginning to pace) Good! I will wait!

*

POET I seem to have lived through this before...

DAUGHTER So do I.

POET Perhaps I dreamed it?

DAUGHTER   Or made it into a poem?

POET   Or made it into a poem.

DAUGHTER   Then you know what poetry is.

POET   Then I know what dreaming is.

DAUGHTER   I feel as if we have stood somewhere else and said these words before.

POET   Then you can soon discover what reality is.

DAUGHTER   Or dreaming.

POET   Or poetry.

*

(The LORD CHANCELLOR, the DEANS OF THE FACULTIES OF THEOLOGY, PHILOSOPHY, MEDICINE, and LAW.)

LORD CHANCELLOR   In the matter of the Door--what is the opinion of the Dean of the Faculty of Theology?

THEOLOGY   I do not have an opinion! I believe...credo...

PHILOSOPHY   I think...

MEDICINE   I know...

LAW   I doubt, until I have evidence and witnesses.

LORD CHANCELLOR   There they go again!... Theology, what do you believe?

THEOLOGY   I believe that this door should not be opened, since it conceals dangerous truths.

PHILOSOPHY   The truth is never dangerous.

MEDICINE   What is truth?

LAW   Whatever can be proved by two witnesses.

THEOLOGY   Two false witnesses can prove anything, with a little "manipulation."

PHILOSOPHY   Truth is wisdom, and wisdom, knowledge, is the essence of philosophy. Philosophy is the science of scientists, the wisdom of wisdoms; all other sciences are the servants of philosophy.

MEDICINE There is no science but natural science. Philosophy is not a science at all. Only empty speculation.

THEOLOGY Hear, hear!

PHILOSOPHY (to THEOLOGY) Hear, hear, indeed! Who do you think you are? You are the mortal enemy of science, you contradict science with ignorance and darkness...

MEDICINE Hear, hear!

THEOLOGY (to MEDICINE) You say hear, hear! You, staring through a magnifying glass and seeing nothing other than the end of your nose! You, with your belief in the treacherous senses, in your eyes, for example, which are just as likely to be long-sighted, short-sighted, blind, purblind, wind-blind, one-eyed, color-blind, red-blind, green-blind...

MEDICINE Blockhead!

THEOLOGY Ass!

(They begin to fight.)

LORD CHANCELLOR Order! Stop picking out each other's eyes; there's nothing to choose between you!

PHILOSOPHY If I had to make a choice between those two, Theology or Medicine, I'd choose--neither!

LAW And if I had to sit in judgment over all three of you, I'd condemn you all, out of hand! You can't agree on a single thing, and have never been able to. Let's get back to business! My Lord, what is your opinion of the door and its opening?

LORD CHANCELLOR Opinion? Oh, I don't have opinions. I am merely a servant of the government, appointed to keep you from tearing each other limb from limb in your attempts to "educate" our youth. Oh no, I'm wary of opinions. I had a few once, but they were pretty soon demolished. Opinions always are: there's always someone who wants to disagree with you. Shall we open this door, even at the risk of revealing dangerous truths?

LAW What is truth? Where is it?

THEOLOGY I am the Truth and the Life...

PHILOSOPHY I am the knowledge of knowledge...

MEDICINE I am exact knowledge...

LAW I doubt...

(They fight.)

*

DAUGHTER   Teachers of youth, be ashamed of yourselves!

LAW   My Lord, as the government's spokesman, and head of our teaching community, denounce this woman's crime! She has told you to be ashamed of yourself; that is impertinence! And in sneering, sarcastic terms, she has described you as a teacher of youth; that is contempt!

DAUGHTER   Oh, poor youth!

LAW   She expresses pity for our youth; in other words, she is finding fault with us! My Lord, denounce her!

DAUGHTER   Yes, I can find fault with you, all of you, for spreading doubt and dissension among the young!

LAW   You see! She casts doubt upon our authority among the young, and accuses us of spreading doubt! I appeal to every respectable man, is not this criminal conduct!

*

RESPECTABLE PEOPLE   Yes, criminal!

LAW   You have been judged by every respectable man! Now, go in peace with your gains, or else...

DAUGHTER   My gains? Or else? Or else what?

LAW   Or else you will be stoned.

POET   Or crucified.

DAUGHTER   I will go. Come with me, and you shall know the answer to the riddle.

POET   What riddle?

DAUGHTER   What did he mean by my gains?

POET   Nothing, probably. It's what we call nonsense. He's simply talking nonsense.

DAUGHTER   But that's what hurt me most.

POET   Of course! That's why he said it. People are like that.

RESPECTABLE PEOPLE   Hurrah! The door is open!

*

LORD CHANCELLOR   What is behind that door?

GLAZIER   I can't see anything.

LORD CHANCELLOR   He can't see anything! I believe that! Deans! What is behind that door?

THEOLOGY   Nothing! That is the solution to the riddle of this world. In the beginning, out of nothing, God created the heavens and the earth.

PHILOSOPHY   Nothing will come of nothing.

MEDICINE   Bosh! That's nothing!

LAW   I have my doubts. There seems to be some mischief here. I appeal to every respectable man.

DAUGHTER (to POET)   Who are the respectable men?

POET   If there's anyone who can answer that, let him! Usually "respectable men" are just one person. Today it could be me, tomorrow it might be you. People are chosen for it; or rather, they elect themselves.

*

RESPECTABLE PEOPLE   Someone has cheated us!

LORD CHANCELLOR   Who has cheated you?

RESPECTABLE PEOPLE   The Daughter!

LORD CHANCELLOR   Will the Daughter please tell us what she means by having this door opened?

DAUGHTER   No, my friends, I will not. If I did you would not believe me.

MEDICINE   That's nothing!

DAUGHTER   Yes, you are right. But you have not understood it.

MEDICINE   What she says is bosh!

ALL   Bosh!

DAUGHTER (to POET)   I pity them.

POET   Do you mean that seriously?

DAUGHTER   I am always serious.

POET   You even pity the respectable people?

DAUGHTER   Perhaps them most of all.

POET   And the four Deans?

DAUGHTER   Them too, and not the least. Four heads, four minds, on one body! Who has created such a monster?

ALL   She refuses to answer!

LORD CHANCELLOR   Then strike her!

DAUGHTER   I have answered.

ALL   Strike her! She answers!

DAUGHTER   Whether I answer or whether I don't: strike her! Come, Seer, I will tell you the riddle; but far away from here, out in the wilderness, where no one can hear us, no one can see us.

*

LAWYER (taking DAUGHTER'S arm)   Have you forgotten your duties?

DAUGHTER   Oh God, no! But I have higher duties.

LAWYER   And your child?

DAUGHTER   My child! What more?

LAWYER   Your child is crying for you.

DAUGHTER   My child! Oh, I am earthbound! And this torment in my breast, this anguish...what is it?

LAWYER   Don't you know?

DAUGHTER   No.

LAWYER   The pangs of conscience!

DAUGHTER   Is this conscience?

A DREAM PLAY

LAWYER Yes, and it will torment you after every unfulfilled duty, after every pleasure, however innocent, if there is such a thing as an innocent pleasure, which is doubtful; after every suffering you cause your neighbor.

DAUGHTER And is there no cure?

LAWYER Yes; but only one. Fulfill your duty!

DAUGHTER You look like a demon when you say that word. What if you have two duties to fulfill?

LAWYER Then you do one first, then the other.

DAUGHTER The highest first...very well: look after my child, for I have my duty to fulfill.

LAWYER Your child is suffering from neglect...would you make someone suffer for your sake?

DAUGHTER My spirit is torn, I am pulled both ways...

LAWYER That's one of the little unpleasantnesses of life.

DAUGHTER I am so divided!

*

POET If you knew the sorrow and misery I have caused by following my vocation, my highest duty, you would not take my hand.

DAUGHTER What have you done?

POET I had a father who built his hopes on me, his only son; he expected me to take over his business. I dropped out of college, and my father worried himself to death. My mother wanted me to be religious; I could not; she disowned me. I had a friend who supported me in hard times; but he wanted to dominate all those I wrote and sang for. To save my own soul I had to strike down my friend and benefactor. Since that time I have never known happiness; people call me base and dishonorable, and it doesn't help that my conscience tells me that I was right, for the very next moment it tells me I was wrong. That's how life is.

*

DAUGHTER Come with me into the wilderness!

LAWYER Your child!

DAUGHTER (indicating everyone) These are my children! Each one of them is a good man, but put them all together and they are devils. Farewell.

*

(Outside the Castle. The same decor as at the beginning of the play. But the ground beneath the castle walls is now scattered with flowers (monkshood). On the summit of the castle roof the crysanthemum is about to bloom. The castle windows are lit with candles.)

*

DAUGHTER Now, with the help of fire, I shall soon return to eternity. This is what you call death, and fear so much.

POET It is fear of the unknown.

DAUGHTER Which you know.

POET Who knows?

DAUGHTER Everyone! Why don't you believe your prophets?

POET No one ever believes prophets. I wonder why. Why is it that people don't believe God when He speaks to them? His power should be irresistible.

DAUGHTER Have you always doubted?

POET No; I have had faith often; but after a little while it faded away as if it were a dream.

DAUGHTER It is not easy to be a human being.

POET You can see that?

DAUGHTER Yes.

POET Tell me, wasn't it Indra who once sent down his son to listen to men's suffering?

DAUGHTER Yes, it was. And how was he received?

POET To answer with a question: how well did he fulfill his mission?

DAUGHTER To answer with another: wasn't human life improved after he came? Tell me the truth.

POET Improved?... Yes, a little; a very little. But, instead of asking questions, will you tell me the riddle?

DAUGHTER Yes; but why? You will not believe me.

POET I will believe you! I know who you are!

DAUGHTER Then I will tell you. In the morning of time, before the creation of the sun, Brahma, the divine source of all things, was seduced by Maja, the mother of this world. This, the mingling of earthly and divine, was the heavenly fall. This world, men, life itself, are merely a phantom, an illusion, a dream...

POET My dream!

DAUGHTER A true dream! To be freed from earthly things, Brahma sought the path of suffering and renunciation. Suffering became the source of redemption. But this longing for suffering conflicts with the will to enjoy life, and to love. Can you understand now what love is, its supreme joy and bitter suffering, its mixture of joy and despair? Can you understand now what woman is? Woman, through whom sin and death entered this world?

POET I understand... And the outcome?

DAUGHTER You already know...the conflict between the pain of pleasure and the pleasure of pain...the suffering of the penitent and the excesses of the sensualist...

POET Always conflict?

DAUGHTER Out of conflict comes energy, just as steam comes from the conflict of water and fire.

POET But what about peace, rest?

DAUGHTER Hush! You may not ask, and I may not answer... The altar is ready for the sacrifice...the flowers stand guard, the candles are lit...white sheets hang in the windows, and the threshold is strewn with pine...

POET You say that so calmly, as if no suffering could come near you.

DAUGHTER I have suffered all your pains a hundredfold, for my senses are finer than yours.

POET Tell me your sorrows!

DAUGHTER Poet, could you tell me yours, so that not a word was lacking; could your words begin to reach my thoughts?

POET No, you are right. To myself I am like a deaf-mute; and when people admired my songs I knew them to be trash, and was ashamed.

DAUGHTER   And yet you wish me to tell you? Look into my eyes.

POET   I cannot meet your gaze...

DAUGHTER   Then how would you endure my words if I should speak?

POET   Yet tell me before you go, what has tormented you most down here?

DAUGHTER   The torment of--being alive. Having my sight weakened by having eyes, my hearing impaired by having ears, my thoughts, my light airy thoughts bound in the fatty labyrinths of the brain. You have seen a brain: what creeping ways, what crooked paths...

POET   That's why respectable men think so crookedly.

DAUGHTER   You are all evil, evil...

POET   How can we be otherwise?

DAUGHTER   Now let me shake the dust from my feet...earth, clay...

(She removes her shoes and places them in the fire.)

*

GATEKEEPER (entering; lays her shawl on the fire)   May I burn my shawl too? (Exit.)

OFFICER   And I my roses; only the stems are left. (Exit.)

BILLSTICKER   These notices may go, but my fishnet--never! (Exit.)

GLAZIER   The diamond which opened the door! Farewell. (Exit.)

LAWYER   The protocol in the matter of the Pope's beard, or the reduction of water at the source of the Ganges. (Exit.)

Q.M.   A small contribution, the black mask which turned me into a blackamoor against my will. (Exit.)

VICTORIA   My beauty, my sorrow. (Exit.)

EDITH   My ugliness, my sorrow. (Exit.)

BLIND MAN (hand in fire)   I give my hand, since I cannot give my eye. (Exit.)

DON JUAN (in wheelchair with COQUETTE and FRIEND)   Hurry, hurry, life is short! (Exeunt.)

*

A DREAM PLAY

POET   I read somewhere that when life nears its end, everyone and everything go by...is this the end?

DAUGHTER   This is my end. Farewell.

POET   Give us some parting word!

DAUGHTER   I cannot! Do you believe that words can express our thoughts?

*

THEOLOGY (entering)   I am disowned by God, persecuted by men, abandoned by the government and despised by my colleagues. How could I have believed what no one else believes? How could I defend a God who will not defend His followers? Everything is bosh! (Throws a book onto the fire. Exits.)

*

POET (retrieving book)   Do you know what this is? A book of martyrs, a calendar with a martyr for every day of the year.

DAUGHTER   Martyr?

POET   Yes; tortured and killed for his belief. Tell me why! Do you believe that everyone who is tortured suffers, and that those who are put to death feel the pain? After all, it is birth that is painful; death comes as a liberator.

*

KRISTIN   I paste, I paste, until there is nothing left to paste...

POET   And if heaven itself cracked open you would try to paste it shut!... Go!

KRISTIN   Aren't there any inner windows in that castle?

POET   No!

KRISTIN   Then I will go! (Exit.)

*

DAUGHTER   Now the end approaches, and it is time to part;

Farewell you human child, you dreamer,
Poet, with best knowledge of the way to live.
Hovering on wings above the earth,
Sometimes you will plunge into the dust,
But to graze it only, never to go under.

Now that I must go, now in the moment of parting,
Leaving a friend and a place,
How everything I have loved rises before me,
How my offences torment me with anguish...
Now I feel all the pain of life,
So this is what it is to be a human being...
Longing for what one has never valued,
Regretting offences one has never committed...
Longing to go and wanting to stay...
The heart torn apart by the steeds of desire,
Rent by indecisiveness, opposition, disharmony...

Farewell! Tell mankind I will remember them,
There, where I am going, and that in your name
I shall bear their lamentations to the throne.
Farewell!

(She goes into the castle. Music. The background is lit by the burning castle, a wall of human faces questioning, sorrowful, despairing. As the castle burns the flower bud on the roof blooms into an enormous chrysanthemum.)